LEMON LAW

CARS IN THE COURTROOM

CECIL C. KUHNE III

Cover design by Cory Ottenwess/ABA Design

Printed in the United States of America.

26 25 24 23 22 5 4 3 2 1

ISBN: 978-1-63905-175-5
e-ISBN: 978-1-63905-176-2

Contents

Introduction

Americans love their cars—and their trucks, vans, and SUVs, too—as clearly shown by how much money they spend on them and by the amount of time and energy they devote to making them shine.

Some 17 million new passenger cars and light trucks are sold every year in the United States, and inevitably, a number of these vehicles arrive at the dealership with irreparable defects in design or workmanship that cause a significant amount of grief to their new owners.

Every state in the country has enacted consumer protection legislation known as lemon laws to assist new vehicle buyers with either recurring mechanical problems (commonly referred to as "warranty nonconformities") in spite of attempts by manufacturers and dealers to repair them or situations where the defects have caused the vehicle to be out of service for a long period of time.

Faced with demands by the consumer, manufacturers and dealers typically have a specified period of time to either exchange the defective vehicles for new ones or refund the consumers' money. Lemon laws are beneficial to consumers because they offer remedies that exceed the limited provisions of vehicle warranties, which might obligate manufacturers to repair vehicles at no cost to consumers but which do not mandate a maximum period of time for completion of repairs or otherwise trigger obligations on behalf of manufacturers and dealers to replace vehicles or refund consumers' money if the repairs cannot be promptly and satisfactorily completed.

Reasonable attempts to repair vehicles are precisely defined by these lemon law statutes. The nonconformities must be presented to manufacturers and dealers for repair a certain number of times, or the vehicles must be out of service for a specified period. If the nonconformities are not then resolved, manufacturers and dealers are required to accept the return of the vehicles and, at the direction of the consumers, either replace the vehicle or refund the full purchase price plus any sales taxes, finance charges, and other costs, less reasonable allowances for use.

The underlying reasons for such lemon laws are clear. The purchase of an automobile is one of the most significant purchases an individual makes. The event can become a nightmare if the automobile does not function properly and the manufacturer or dealer is unable or unwilling to remedy the situation.

Lemon laws vary slightly from state to state, but most states define a warranty nonconformity as "any defect or condition that substantially impairs the use, value, or safety of a motor vehicle to the consumer and does not conform to the express warranty of the manufacturer or distributor."

These remedial statutes prescribe in some detail (1) the obligations of consumers to attempt to resolve the vehicle's problems promptly (say, within a year or 18,000 miles) after taking delivery of the vehicle; (2) the number of times consumers must take the vehicle to the shop for repair (say, three times for each nonconformity or eight times for all nonconformities); and (3) the number of days the vehicle has been in the shop (say, 30 days) to be considered a lemon. An example follows:

> It shall be presumed that *a reasonable number of attempts* have been undertaken by the manufacturer, its dealer, or its authorized agent *to conform* a motor vehicle to any *applicable express warranty* if, during the period of *one year* following the date of original delivery or during the first *18,000 miles* of operation, whichever is earlier, any of the following apply:
>
> **(A)** Substantially the *same nonconformity* has been subject to repair *three or more times* and either continues to exist or recurs;
>
> **(B)** The vehicle is *out of service* by reason of repair for a cumulative total of *30 or more calendar days*;
>
> **(C)** There have been *eight or more attempts* to repair *any nonconformity*;
>
> **(D)** There has been *at least one attempt* to repair a nonconformity that results in a condition that is likely to cause *death or serious bodily injury* if the vehicle is driven, and the nonconformity either continues to exist or recurs. (Emphasis added)

Lemon law statutes then generally provide that if the vehicle cannot be repaired, the consumer must contact the manufacturer or dealer and request that the vehicle be replaced or their money refunded:

(A) If a new motor vehicle *does not conform* to any applicable express warranty and the consumer *reports the nonconformity* to the manufacturer, its agent, or its authorized dealer during the period of one year following the date of original delivery or during the first 18,000 miles of operation, whichever is earlier, the manufacturer, its agent, or its authorized *dealer shall make any repairs as are necessary to conform the vehicle to such express warranty*, notwithstanding the fact that the repairs are made after the expiration of the appropriate time period.

(B) If the manufacturer, its agent, or its authorized dealer is *unable to conform the motor vehicle to any applicable express warranty* by repairing or correcting any nonconformity after a reasonable number of repair attempts, the manufacturer, at the consumer's option, *either* shall *replace the motor vehicle with a new motor vehicle* acceptable to the *consumer or shall accept return of the vehicle* from the consumer and *refund each of the following*:

(1) The *full purchase price*;

(2) All *incidental damages*, including, but not limited to, any fees charged by the lender or lessor for making or canceling the loan or lease, and any expenses incurred by the consumer as a result of the nonconformity, such as charges for towing, vehicle rental, meals, and lodging. (Emphasis added)

As straightforward as lemon laws appear, a surprising number of very interesting—and sometimes complex—legal issues arise, leading to a substantial amount of litigation (numerous firms around the country specialize exclusively in lemon law cases). Such thorny legal issues include:

- Is substantial impairment of the defective vehicle "to the consumer" to be judged as an objective test or a subjective one?
- Must the consumer be completely unaware of the noncomformity before accepting delivery of the vehicle?

- How specific must the consumer be in notifying the manufacturer or dealer of the consumer's selection of the remedy to either replace or buy back the defective vehicle?
- Must all accessories of a vehicle replaced pursuant to the lemon law also be brand new, even if not defective?
- Can the consumer be required to sign a general release in order to receive the remedies afforded by the lemon law?
- Do negotiations between the consumer and the manufacturer or dealer toll the time in which the manufacturer must replace or buy back the defective vehicle?
- Is the manufacturer or dealer allowed more time to replace or buy back the defective vehicle if the consumer is engaged in obstructive tactics?
- Where is the line between personal and business use of the vehicle which makes the vehicle ineligible for lemon law enforcement?
- Are leased vehicles covered under lemon laws, and if so, how is the transfer of the vehicle's title handled?
- Do lemon laws apply to demonstrators, motor homes, and motorcycles?

The lemon law arena is of course governed by the respective statutes, with most states following much the same format and philosophy. The statutory framework has also led to surprisingly consistent treatment by the courts. Naturally, the jurisprudence of every state constantly evolves and has to be consulted by practitioners to determine how the courts are currently interpreting the statutes.

Rather than a dry recitation of legislative provisions, this book places the law in the context of actual controversies, lending to its practicality for those engaged in the area. Each chapter is preceded by "practice pointers," and the text is organized logically to follow the progression and development of litigation claims.

My hope is that this collection of cases and practice tips will prove to be a useful reference for those entering the fascinating automotive fray between manufacturers, dealers, leasing companies, and consumers.

1

Proving Warranty Nonconformity

PRACTICE POINTER

Lemon law statutes are drafted to be specific in the actions they require of consumers in controversies with manufacturers and dealers over vehicle warranties. In the case that follows–*Neeld v. American Isuzu Motors, Inc.*, 2004 WL 2715919 (Ohio)–the consumer of a vehicle suspected to be a lemon has clearly defined obligations, and failure to meet these obligations will impair the consumer's remedies.

The consumer must not only report and document vehicle defects (known as "warranty nonconformities") to the manufacturer or dealership, but also must then attempt to have those problems resolved as soon as possible, and certainly within the time and mileage requirements specified in the statute.

A warranty nonconformity under most lemon laws is defined as "a defect or condition" that substantially impairs the *use, value, or safety* of a motor vehicle to the consumer and *does not conform to the express warranty* of the manufacturer or distributor.

To properly present a lemon law claim, the consumer must provide the manufacturer or dealer with the opportunity to repair the vehicle's nonconformity. The manufacturer or dealer must undertake a *reasonable number of attempts to conform a motor vehicle to any applicable express warranty.*

The statutes vary from state to state, but most commonly, they include the following requirements: the manufacturer or dealer must have tried to repair the "*substantially same nonconformity*" of the vehicle *three or more times* without success; *eight or more attempts* must be made to repair "any nonconformity"; at least one attempt is required to repair a nonconformity that results in a condition that is "*likely to cause death or serious bodily injury*" if the vehicle is driven; or the vehicle must have been out of service for a cumulative total of *30 or more calendar days*.

Most lemon laws then provide specific remedies for the consumer. If a new motor vehicle *does not conform to the warranty and the consumer reports the nonconformity* to the manufacturer or dealer during the applicable period (say, *one year* following the date of original delivery or during the first 18,000 miles of operation, whichever is earlier), the manufacturer or dealer *must make any necessary repairs to conform the vehicle to such express warranty*.

If the manufacturer or dealer is *unable* to conform the motor vehicle to the warranty by repairing the nonconformity, the manufacturer or dealer, *at the consumer's option*, either shall *replace the motor vehicle with a new motor vehicle* acceptable to the consumer or shall *accept return of the vehicle from the consumer and refund the full purchase price and all incidental damages and expenses*.

The more specific the consumer can be in describing the warranty nonconformities and in detailing what is needed to repair them, the better. This is shown by the following case, where the consumer provided the detailed evidence necessary to have a successful claim.

A consumer named Joseph Neeld sued Isuzu Motors under the state's lemon law for his lease of a brand-new 2001 Isuzu Rodeo, a midsize SUV.

Neeld alleged that the manufacturer, Isuzu, failed to repair various defects in the vehicle, which in the lemon law world are formally known as "warranty nonconformities." Among the car's many problems were the following:

- A badly slipping transmission,
- Loud popping noises in the engine,
- Disconcerting creaks in the car's rear end,
- Annoying squeaks in the driver's door,

- Pesky vibrations in the steering wheel, and
- Odd rubbing noises in the steering column.

Within 12 months of his lease of the Rodeo and before it had been driven 18,000 miles, Neeld brought the SUV to several different Isuzu dealerships for repair. Many of the vehicle's issues were eventually resolved, but unfortunately the slipping transmission and the various knocking motor noises remained.

In fact, the Rodeo's engine noises continued long after the initial 12 months and 18,000 miles, and on November 6, 2002, the dealer finally took the dramatic measure of replacing the short block of the engine. This major repair resolved most of the engine issues, but some of the steering noises and transmission problems continued, despite the fact that the vehicle had been in the service departments of various Isuzu dealerships for a total of 44 days.

Neeld finally sued Isuzu for violation of the state's lemon law. At trial, Neeld presented the testimony of an expert witness named William Beltzer, who had 35 years' experience as an automobile mechanic, service supervisor, and independent diagnostic expert. Beltzer identified two principal problems with the Rodeo.

The most readily identifiable issue with the car, Beltzer reported, was "flare shift," a condition in which, as the automatic transmission shifts, the tachometer reveals a sudden and dramatic increase in engine speed, followed by a sudden drop. This reading, Belzer said, typically indicates a transmission clutch or friction band that is not engaging at the correct time, and that the defect could lead to premature clutch failure and eventually the need to replace the transmission (at a cost of about $4,300).

Beltzer also pointed to a serious defect in the transmission and stated that it was not the result of any abuse or neglect by the consumer. In the court hearing, Beltzer gave testimony regarding the knocking in the engine and the subsequent short block replacement:

> ***Q:*** If there was an engine—I'm going to give you a hypothetical here, but you have got a vehicle which has a knocking or popping sound which is consistent over time and eventually increases in nature and eventually a portion of the engine is replaced, and that noise is no longer there, would you be able to, within a reasonable degree of professional certainty in the automobile industry, draw a causal relationship between the noise and the engine that was replaced?

A: Well, I would say with a high degree of probability that the knock, whatever the knock was, was something out of a tolerance problem to begin with. Normally, engines don't knock. They have clicking noises from fuel injectors, and they have pulleys that occasionally rattle. There are belt noises that you can hear at certain times, but knocking is not a common noise in an engine. And if there is a knock—and I have seen myself a knocking on and on and on for a long period of time, and suddenly you get an engine failure. That's not unusual.

Q: A knocking sound like you are describing is a symptom of some larger problem?

A: Yeah, it is a—
MR. SCHISLER [counsel for the defendant Isuzu]: Objection, your Honor. Leading.
THE COURT: Sustained.

Q: (BY MR. LUXENBURG [counsel for the plaintiff Neeld]) Is the knocking sound a symptom of a larger problem?

A: Well, as I stated earlier, knocking is normally due to a tolerance problem where something has got too much gap in it, too great of a tolerance to maintain a quiet, smooth operating engine. Most of the time it is found in the bearings and connecting rod area with the crankshaft. Now, occasionally, to a lesser degree, you will see pistons that don't fit the cylinder walls properly, and they will knock; they will make a knocking type noise as well.

In support of his case, Neeld presented to the court receipts showing that the warranty repairs for the Rodeo totaled over $6,000 within the first 33,000 miles and that most of these expenses related to his previous complaints about the car. This $6,000 sum did not include the potential expenditure for a new transmission. Neeld testified at trial that, due to the incessant problems with the Rodeo, he was simply forced to buy another vehicle.

The evidence, then, was clear that Neeld complained of persistent transmission problems early and often in his ownership of the Rodeo, and certainly well within the 12-month or 18,000-mile limit required by the statute. Neeld's expert diagnosed the probable cause of this ongoing problem with some specificity, speculating that the "flare shift" condition would likely lead to early transmission failure and substantially impair the vehicle's value. The expert also testified that the sums expended on warranty repairs, as well as the nature of those repairs (including the short block replacement), would serve as a red flag to any potential buyer of the vehicle.

The Isuzu company rebutted Neeld's case with expert testimony alleging the absence of any serious nonconformity in the vehicle and advancing alternative theories for Neeld's complaints. It even suggested that the problems were the result of Neeld driving the car far greater distances than the lease allowed. This high mileage usage, in and of itself, Isuzu contended, demonstrated that Neeld had not suffered any impairment in the normal use of the vehicle.

The court first took a close look at the state's lemon law statute, which defined nonconformity as "any defect or condition that substantially impairs the *use, value, or safety* of a motor vehicle to the consumer and *does not conform to the express warranty* of the manufacturer or distributor" (emphasis added).

The trial court was thus faced with the question of whether the consumer's allegations met the elements of a lemon law claim, which were clearly set forth in the statute.:

> It shall be presumed that *a reasonable number of attempts have been undertaken* by the manufacturer, its dealer, or its authorized agent to *conform a motor vehicle to any applicable express warranty* if, during the period of *one year* following the date of original delivery or during the first *18,000 miles* of operation, whichever is earlier, any of the following apply:
>
> **(A)** Substantially the same nonconformity has been subject to *repair three or more times* and either continues to exist or recurs;
>
> **(B)** The vehicle is out of service by reason of repair for a cumulative total of *30 or more calendar days*;
>
> **(C)** There have been *eight or more attempts* to repair any nonconformity;
>
> **(D)** There has been at least one attempt to repair a nonconformity that results in a condition that is *likely to cause death or serious bodily injury* if the vehicle is driven, and the nonconformity either continues to exist or recurs. (Emphasis added)

The lemon law statute then provided the following remedies for the consumer of a nonconforming vehicle:

(A) If a new motor vehicle *does not conform to any applicable express warranty and the consumer reports the nonconformity* to the manufacturer, its agent, or its authorized dealer during the period of *one year* following the date of original delivery or during the first *18,000 miles* of operation, whichever is earlier, the manufacturer, its agent, or its authorized dealer *shall make any repairs as are necessary to conform the vehicle to such express warranty*, notwithstanding the fact that the repairs are made after the expiration of the appropriate time period.

(B) If the manufacturer, its agent, or its authorized dealer is *unable to conform the motor vehicle* to any applicable express warranty by repairing or correcting any nonconformity after a reasonable number of repair attempts, the manufacturer, *at the consumer's option*, <u>either</u> shall *replace the motor vehicle* with a new motor vehicle acceptable to the consumer *or* shall *accept return of the vehicle* from the consumer and refund each of the following:

(1) The *full purchase price*;

(2) All *incidental damages*, including, but not limited to, any fees charged by the lender or lessor for making or canceling the loan or lease, and any expenses incurred by the consumer as a result of the nonconformity, such as charges for towing, vehicle rental, meals, and lodging. (Emphasis added)

After carefully deliberating the evidence presented by the parties, the jury returned a verdict in favor of Neeld, finding that Neeld had *not* demonstrated a substantial impairment of the vehicle's use or safety, but that he had shown a substantial impairment of the vehicle's value.

The appellate court affirmed the decision of the trial court, with the following declarations:

- The evidence presented by Neeld regarding the transmission defect, engine knock, and potential engine failure was sufficient for reasonable minds to conclude that a warranty nonconformity in the vehicle existed,

- These warranty nonconformities were brought to the attention of dealer service departments within the 12-month and 18,000-mile period of the lemon law statute, and
- The resale value of the vehicle would be significantly impaired by the remaining transmission defect.

At long last, then, Mr. Neeld's beloved Isuzu Rodeo—complete with its steady stream of troublesome knocking sounds and errant transmission shifting—was officially and irrevocably declared to be a lemon.

2

What Constitutes Defective

PRACTICE POINTER

To be classified as a lemon, a problem with a vehicle must, under the terms of most lemon law statutes, "substantially impair the use, safety, or value of the vehicle."

This definition would necessarily *exclude minor "fit and finish" problems considered to be more cosmetic than those affecting the engine, drivetrain, or mechanical functioning of the vehicle.* The case that follows involves adjustments to the car's moldings, windows, bumpers, and headlights, which did not qualify the vehicle's replacement or refund under lemon law.

Even assuming for a moment that these problems satisfied the provisions of the lemon law, the consumer in the following case—*General Motors Acceptance Corporation v. Hollanshead*, 663 N.E.2d 663 (Ohio 1995)—did not prove that an individual nonconformity had been presented to the dealership on three or more occasions that the consumer brought the car to the dealership.

In fact, it appears that the consumer had given the dealer only *one* opportunity to inspect the car and *no* opportunity to actually repair it. Thus, the consumer had *not* established that the manufacturer/dealer had not undertaken a reasonable number of repair attempts.

Furthermore, the consumer had *not* provided evidence demonstrating that any of the other statutory presumptions concerning a reasonable number of repair attempts applied to her case.

The moral for consumers is clear: the nonconformity must be of a nature involving "use, safety, or value" to qualify, and the nonconformity must be presented to the dealership for repair the requisite number of times under the statute.

Linda Hollanshead leased a beautiful new 1992 Cadillac Eldorado from McDaniel Motors Company in Marion, Ohio, and she immediately began to notice numerous so-called fit and finish issues in this expensive car, which required minor adjustments to the car's moldings, windows, bumpers, and headlights.

Admittedly, none of these unsightly, and sometimes irritating, issues affected the engine, drivetrain, and mechanical functioning of the Eldorado, but as a result of these cosmetic blemishes, Hollanshead decided to stop making car payments to General Motors Acceptance Corporation (GMAC), the assignee of the lease.

In due time, GMAC filed a complaint to recover possession of the Eldorado from Hollanshead, who then filed (1) a counterclaim against GMAC asserting that the vehicle was a nonconforming new motor vehicle, and (2) a third-party complaint against Cadillac/General Motors Corporation (GMC) and McDaniel Motors for breach of warranty and violation of the state's lemon law.

In the succeeding trial, the court—concluding that the lemon law was inapplicable to *lessees* of new motor vehicles—entered summary judgment in favor of McDaniel Motors as the dealer and summary judgment in favor of Cadillac/GMC as the manufacturer for the breach of warranty and lemon law claims.

Under the provisions of the state's lemon law, a "consumer" was defined as "the purchaser, other than for purposes of resale, of a motor vehicle," and:

> . . . any person to whom the motor vehicle is transferred during the duration of the express warranty that is applicable to the motor vehicle, *and any other person who is entitled by the terms of the warranty to enforce the warranty.* (Emphasis added)

As for the class of individuals entitled to bring a civil action for a nonconforming vehicle, the lemon law provided that:

> Any *purchaser* of a new motor vehicle who suffers *any loss due to nonconformity* of the motor vehicle as a result of failure by the manufacturer, its agent, or its authorized dealer to comply with the statute *may bring a civil action* in a court of common pleas. (Emphasis added)

As for the remedies available to consumers of nonconforming vehicles, the statute provided that:

(A) If a new motor vehicle *does not conform to any applicable express warranty* and *the consumer reports the nonconformity* to the manufacturer, its agent, or its authorized dealer during the period of *one year* following the date of original delivery or during the first *18,000* miles of operation, whichever is earlier, the manufacturer, its agent, or its authorized dealer shall *make any repairs as are necessary* to conform the vehicle to such express warranty, notwithstanding the fact that the repairs are made after the expiration of the appropriate time period.

(B) If the manufacturer, its agent, or its authorized dealer is *unable to conform the motor vehicle* to any applicable express warranty by repairing or correcting any defect or condition that substantially impairs the use, safety, or value of the motor vehicle to the consumer after a reasonable number of repair attempts, the manufacturer shall, at the consumer's option, replace the motor vehicle with a new motor vehicle acceptable to the consumer or accept return of the vehicle from the consumer and refund each of the following:

- **(1)** The *full purchase price* including, but not limited to, charges for undercoating, transportation, and installed options;
- **(2)** All *collateral charges*, including but not limited to, sales tax, license and registration fees, and similar government charges;
- **(3)** All *finance charges* incurred by the consumer;
- **(4)** All *incidental damages*, including any reasonable fees charged by the lender for making or canceling the loan." (Emphasis added)

Hollanshead appealed the summary judgments, where the question was a straightforward one: whether a lessee was a "consumer" under the lemon law and therefore entitled to protection of the statute.

The first appellate court in the state to ever consider the issue of whether a lessee was a consumer had held that the class of individuals defined as "consumers" *did* include "nonpurchasers" and "nontitle-holders" as those entitled to enforce the vehicle's warranty. The court in that seminal case concluded that lessees were the class of consumers that most closely fit this category, and thus lessees were entitled to relief under the law.

The present appellate court agreed, reasoning that the lemon law was a consumer protection statute that should be liberally construed. The court found that sound public policy dictated that lessees—many of whom had made substantial advance payments under lease agreements and many of whom had paid a variety of "service charges," such as "interest" and even "sales tax"—should be afforded the same basic protection as purchasers of new automobiles.

On the other hand, the present appellate court did express some reservations about applying the law to lessees. The remedies set forth in the lemon law statute specifically described a consumer who had actually *purchased* and received title to a new motor vehicle. Additionally, most lease transactions contained no reference to any of the refundable items described in the lemon law. Applying the statute law remedies to a lessee, the court conceded, would in effect require "rewriting" the statute.

Nonetheless, even if the lemon law was applied to lessees as a class, the court did not believe that in the present case Hollanshead had established the facts necessary to entitle her to relief under the law.

In order for Hollanshead to prevail on her claim, she had to prove that there was a defect that substantially impaired "the use, value, or safety" of the motor vehicle. The repairs performed on Hollanshead's car consisted of "fit and finish" adjustments to the moldings, windows, bumpers, and headlights of the car. Hollanshead admitted that there were absolutely *no* mechanical problems with the automobile.

Even assuming *arguendo*—a big stretch—that the defects in Hollanshead's vehicle could be considered to "substantially impair the use, safety, or value of the vehicle," Hollanshead's claim would still fail because (1) neither Cadillac/GMC nor the dealer had been given ample opportunity to repair the vehicle, and (2) Hollanshead had not proved that the defects persisted after the manufacturer or dealer had made reasonable attempts to repair the problems.

With respect to what exactly constituted a reasonable number of repair attempts, the lemon law statute provided the following:

> It shall be presumed that *a reasonable number of attempts* have been undertaken by the manufacturer, its dealer, or its authorized agent *to conform a motor vehicle to any applicable express warranty* if, during the period of one year following the date of original delivery or during the first 18,000 miles of operation, whichever is earlier, any of the following apply:
>
> **(A)** Substantially the same nonconformity has been *subject to repair three or more times* and continues to exist;
>
> **(B)** The vehicle is out of service by reason of repair for a cumulative total of *30 or more calendar days*;
>
> **(C)** There have been *eight or more attempts* to repair any nonconformity that substantially impairs the use and value of the motor vehicle to the consumer;
>
> **(D)** There has been at least one attempt to repair a nonconformity that results in a condition that is *likely to cause death or serious bodily injury* if the vehicle is driven, and the nonconformity continues to exist. (Emphasis added)

It was clear, then, that no individual nonconformity had been presented on the three or more occasions that Hollanshead brought the car to the dealership. In fact, it appeared at trial that Hollanshead had given GMC/Cadillac only *one* opportunity to inspect the car and *no* opportunity to actually repair it.

Thus, Hollanshead had *not* established that a reasonable number of repair attempts had been undertaken by Cadillac/GMC or McDaniel Motors. Furthermore, Hollanshead had *not* provided evidence demonstrating that any of the other three statutory presumptions concerning a reasonable number of repair attempts applied to her case.

The summary judgment in favor of Cadillac/GMC was thus affirmed and to the relief of Eldorado owners everywhere, Ms. Hollanshead's expensive exemplar—even with all of its annoying, loose-fitting trim—was officially and undeniably declared *not* to be a lemon.

3

Obligations of the Consumer

Practice Pointer

Under the provisions of most lemon laws, the consumer of a problematic vehicle must report those warranty problems to the manufacturer or authorized dealership—and not unauthorized mechanics—within the time required by the statute, and *the vehicle must actually be presented to the authorized dealer for repairs. Careful documentation of these events to the authorized dealer is critical* to meet the requirements of the statute.

Furthermore, by their terms, lemon laws impose liability on the "manufacturer, its dealer, or its authorized agent" of the motor vehicle. The term *manufacturer* is typically defined in the lemon law statute as a company that "manufactures, assembles, or imports motor vehicles." The *manufacturer of component parts, including engines, does* not *fit into any of these descriptions.*

In the case that follows—*Temple v. Fleetwood Enterprises, Inc.*, 133 Fed.Appx. 254 (6th Cir. 2005)—the consumer could raise their claims only against the vehicle manufacturer and not the engine manufacturer since the statute imposed liability on the "manufacturer, its dealer, or its authorized agent" of the "motor vehicle."

Moreover, the statute's remedy requiring replacement of the vehicle or refund of the purchase price is designed to be used against the final manufacturer of a vehicle. Under the language of the statute, the courts are not "required to determine which manufacturer among all the component parts manufacturers is responsible for the defect that renders the vehicle nonconforming."

On March 12, 1998, Brenda and Glen Temple purchased a 1998 Fleetwood motor home from Avalon R.V. Center. The motor home contained an engine manufactured by Cummins Engine Company, and the vehicle was assembled by Fleetwood Motor Homes of Indiana, which warranted the vehicle.

The Temples operated the motor home for about three and a half years when, in early October 2001, they finally abandoned the problematic vehicle at a Fleetwood repair shop in Decatur, Indiana, and subsequently filed suit under the lemon law.

The key period under the warranty for complaints to the manufacturer was the first year of ownership. The one-year period ended on March 12, 1999. The following is a summary of the numerous issues the Temples experienced during that period:

- **March 1998 through May 1998.** The Temples noted in their "Complaint History" that they had problems with: stove burners, the heating and air conditioning system, water leakage, the awning support arms, the power control box, and the television set. These problems were not reported to Fleetwood or the Avalon dealership, and there were no attempts to repair the problems until the Temples finally brought the motor home to a Fleetwood dealer.
- **June 1998.** The Temples complained for the first time to the Avalon dealership about problems with the electronic control panel, wiring problems, and the HVAC. The Temples also complained about: the leaking windshield, the defrost vent, the noisy water pump, the broken towel holder, a missing bolt on the front storage compartment, and rust spots. Sometime in July 1998, the Temples complained to Avalon about the power control box. The dealership repaired all of these problems.
- **December 1998.** The Temples noted in their Complaint History: a potential oil and fuel leak, broken molding in the bedroom, a

loose wall mirror in the galley, dangling bedroom drawers, and poor refrigerator seals. These issues were not reported to Fleetwood or Avalon.

- **January 1999.** The Temples brought the motor home to Avalon to be cleaned and have the awning reinstalled, services that Avalon completed at no charge. The Temples later complained to an unauthorized dealer about problems with the HVAC unit. However, the dealer did not fix the problem because it could not work on Fleetwood motor homes.
- **February 1999.** The Temples' Complaint History noted that the brake lights and turn signals were inoperable, but the Temples could not get an appointment and fixed the fuse problem themselves. Sometime in March 1999, the Temples again complained to an unauthorized dealer about problems with the HVAC unit.
- **March 1999.** The Complaint History noted that the Temples brought the motor home to another dealer to install air vent covers and a splash guard and to tighten the awning springs.

Now, to the provisions of the Fleetwood new motor home warranty, which stated (*emphasis added*):

Limited One–Year/Three–Year Warranty Coverage Provided

Your new motor home, including the structure, plumbing, heating and electrical systems, and all appliances and equipment installed by the manufacturer, is warranted under normal use to be *free from manufacturing defects in material or workmanship*. Defects or damage to paint, graphics, exterior materials, upholstery or other appearance items that may occur prior to delivery are usually corrected during the inspection process at the manufacturing plant or the dealership.

The warranty extends to the first retail purchaser and his transferee(s) and begins on the date of original retail delivery or the date the motor home is first placed into service as a rental, commercial or demonstrator unit (whichever occurs first). The warranty extends for the following periods:

1. For all defects (other than structural) the warranty extends for a period *of one year from such date or until the unit has received 15,000 total miles* of use as determined by the mileage shown on the odometer (whichever occurs first). . . .

WHEN THE DEALER DOES NOT RESOLVE THE PROBLEM:

If the dealer is unable or unwilling to resolve a problem which the owner is convinced is covered by the warranty, he should *contact the manufacturing plant at the address listed and provide the manufacturer with a description in writing of the problem and attempts made to resolve it.*

MANUFACTURING PLANT OBLIGATIONS:

Upon receipt of notice of a claim, where the dealer was unable or unwilling to resolve the problem, the manufacturing plant will repair or replace any parts necessary to correct defects in material or workmanship or will take other appropriate action as may be required. . . .

WHAT IS NOT COVERED BY THE EXPRESS WARRANTY:

THIS WARRANTY DOES NOT COVER:

1. The automotive system (including the chassis and drive train), tires and batteries, which are covered by the separate warranties of the respective manufacturers of these components. . . .

   The manufacturer is not responsible for any undertaking, representation or warranty made by any dealer or other person beyond those expressly set forth in this warranty. . . .

In addition to this Fleetwood warranty, the motor home was also covered by a Cummins Base Engine Warranty that provided:

> The Base Engine Warranty covers any failures of the Engine which result, under normal use and service, from a defect in material or factory workmanship (Warrantable Failure). This coverage begins with the sale of the Engine by Cummins and continues for *seven years or 150,000 miles*, whichever occurs first, from the date of delivery of the Engine to the first user. (Emphasis added)

The key period for the Cummins engine warranty was the first seven years of ownership or the first 150,000 miles. The Temples brought the motor home back to Cummins for a total of six repairs to the engine:

(1) **February 1999.** During the first year of ownership, the Temples complained of a potential oil and fuel leak to an authorized Cummins dealer. The dealer found only two oil leaks, which the dealer then repaired at no charge under the Cummins warranty.

(2) **March 1999.** The Temples complained about a fuel leak to another authorized Cummins dealer. That dealer found a fuel leak in the No. 5 injector fuel line and fixed the problem. The dealer also replaced a fuse to fix a problem with the engine brake.

(3) **March 2000.** The Temples complained of a problem with the engine's oil pressure sensor. It was repaired under the Cummins warranty.

(4) **March 2001.** The Temples complained again of a problem with the engine's oil pressure sensor. It was repaired by the same dealer under the Cummins warranty.

(5) **March 2001.** A fuel leak developed in the # 5 fuel injector line. This was the same fuel injector line that had been repaired two years earlier. A Cummins dealer repaired the problem under the warranty.

(6) **July 2001.** The Motor Home broke down. Another Cummins dealer discovered that the No. 4 fuel injector was cracked and repaired it under the warranty.

Finally, the Temples had had enough, and they left the motor home at a Fleetwood repair shop in Decatur, Indiana, sometime in October 2001.

The Temples' expert, Professor Louis Boehman, inspected the motor home on three occasions. After conducting the first inspection, Boehman produced an expert report that did not reach a final conclusion but called for further examination. Boehman stated that "the motor home is unsafe to drive until a top notch diesel technician, Cummins trained, goes through and checks out the entire fuel system."

After the second inspection and road test, Boehman then produced a supplemental expert report in which he concluded that "during and after the test drive, it was noted by all present that on this occasion the high pressure fuel supply lines did not leak."

Boehman did note, however, that the 30-mile "very mild" road test was not sufficient to test the engine's ability and that the conclusion of the manufacturer's expert that the engine had a "clean bill of health" was inappropriate in light of the fact that at the end of the road test, both experts had noted a "small" oil leak.

In an affidavit, Boehman offered conclusory opinions that:

(1) The engine had "problems" that "caused the engine to break down on four separate occasions,"
(2) The engine "problems" "were not repaired within a reasonable number of attempts,"
(3) The engine's "oil pressure sending units" were "defective" due to "a defect in the manufacturing of" the motor home,
(4) An oil leak was "the direct result of the engine oil pressure sending units not being properly repaired within a reasonable number of attempts,"
(5) "High-pressure engine fuel lines should never exhibit problems during the life of an engine,"
(6) The fuel line problem, "if uncorrected," will "substantially impair the safety of the motor home" and will "impair its use and value to any reasonable consumer," and
(7) The road test was "completely inadequate to reveal the existence of oil and fuel leak defects."

During his deposition, Boehman admitted that he had never performed any tests or measurements on the engine. Despite this admission in his deposition, Boehman claimed that the opinions expressed in his affidavit revealed "a reasonable degree of engineering certainty," based on his "education, training, and experience."

The appellate court noted that the lemon law placed a duty on the manufacturer of a new motor vehicle to "make any repairs as are necessary to conform the vehicle to its express warranty" within the first year, or 18,000 miles, whichever occurred first. The Complaint History revealed that the motor home was driven 18,000 miles sometime in March 2000—*after* the first anniversary of ownership. Thus, the requisite timeframe for making a lemon law claim had expired on March 12, 1999.

The state lemon law contained a section entitled "Presumptions," which set forth four definitive methods by which a consumer could satisfy "a reasonable number of attempts" to repair the vehicle:

> It shall be *presumed that a reasonable number of attempts have been undertaken* by the manufacturer, its dealer, or its authorized agent to conform a motor vehicle to any applicable express warranty if, during the period of one year following the date of original delivery or during the first *18,0000 miles* of operation, whichever is earlier, any of the following apply:
>
> **(A)** Substantially the same nonconformity has been *subject to repair three or more times* and either continues to exist or recurs;
>
> **(B)** The vehicle is out of service by reason of repair for a cumulative total of *30 or more calendar days*;
>
> **(C)** There have been *eight or more attempts* to repair any nonconformity;
>
> **(D)** There has been at least one attempt to repair a nonconformity that results in a condition that is likely to cause *death or serious bodily injury* if the vehicle is driven, and the nonconformity either continues to exist or recurs. (Emphasis added)

Furthermore, the statute provided consumers with a simple remedy should the manufacturer fail to repair the vehicle within a reasonable number of attempts):

> If the manufacturer, its agent, or its authorized dealer is *unable to conform* the motor vehicle to any applicable express warranty *by repairing or correcting any nonconformity* after *a reasonable number of repair attempts*, the manufacturer, *at the consumer's option, either* shall *replace the motor vehicle* with a new motor vehicle acceptable to the consumer *or* shall accept return of the vehicle from the consumer and refund each of the following:
>
> **(1)** The *full purchase price*;
>
> **(2)** *All incidental damages*, including, but not limited to, any fees charged by the lender or lessor for making or canceling the loan or lease, and any expenses incurred by the consumer as a result of the nonconformity, such as charges for towing, vehicle rental, meals, and lodging. (Emphasis added)

Ultimately, the trial court determined that the number of service repairs performed by both Fleetwood and Cummins during the first year of ownership did *not* meet any of the statutory elements requiring at least three repairs to the same nonconformity.

The Temples argued that they complained about the HVAC problems three times to three different dealers and that the problem was never repaired. But the court pointed out that the HVAC problem was repaired only *one* time. The fact that the Temples sought repair from three different dealers for the HVAC problem did not meet the statutory presumption, as two of the three dealers were not authorized to work on Fleetwood motor homes.

The Temples also contended that their motor home had 12 different defects that were covered by the lemon law. But the court found that only six defects occurred during the lemon law timeframe, and thus the Temples failed to meet the statutory presumption that Fleetwood or Cummins repair "any nonconformity" eight or more times.

The Temples finally argued that the No. 5 fuel injector leak constituted a deadly defect that met the lemon law definition of "a nonconformity that results in a condition that is likely to cause death or serious bodily injury if the vehicle is driven, and the nonconformity either continues to exist or recurs." Their only evidence, however, was a bald assertion by Mr. Temple, and the court ruled that this testimony failed to provide appropriate evidence of a deadly defect.

Furthermore, the court also held that the Temples could raise their claim only against the vehicle manufacturer and not the engine manufacturer since the statute imposed liability on the "manufacturer, its dealer, or its authorized agent" of the "motor vehicle."

The term *manufacturer* was defined as a "person who manufactures, assembles, or imports motor vehicles, including motor homes." Cummins, the manufacturer of the engine, did not fit into any of these descriptions.

Moreover, the statute's remedy requiring replacement of the vehicle or refund of the purchase price was designed to be used against the final manufacturer of a vehicle. Under the language of the statute, the courts were not "required to determine which manufacturer among all the component parts manufacturers is responsible for the defect which renders the vehicle nonconforming."

The court also noted that the final manufacturer was not left without remedy, for the manufacturer had recourse against the manufacturers of component parts for providing defective products should the manufacturer be sued by a consumer under the lemon law.

Much to the dismay of the Temples, the summary judgment in favor of Fleetwood was affirmed in all respects. And while the Temples were left with a motor home full of unresolved problems, they did have a very detailed log of their complaints about the vehicle.

4

Notice of Deficiency

PRACTICE POINTER

The notice required by a disgruntled consumer to the manufacturer or dealer of a lemon vehicle is clearly specified in the statute, and it must be strictly followed. The lemon law clearly provides that the manufacturer "shall carry out the requirement" and that "At the direction of a consumer, the manufacturer do one of the following. . . ."

The specific remedy requested—whether it is a *vehicle replacement or a refund—must be clearly identified to the manufacturer or dealer*, and the willingness of the consumer to transfer *title* to the vehicle to the manufacturer or dealer must be *explicitly* stated.

Otherwise, *the consumer's notice to the manufacturer or dealer is fatally defective and the claim under the lemon law fails.*

In the case that is the subject of this chapter—*Berends v. Mack Truck, Inc.*, 643 N.W.2d 158 (Wis. 2002)—the consumer's action is premised on an allegation that the manufacturer failed to provide the consumer with a comparable new motor vehicle. The manufacturer argued that because the consumer's notice was defective, there was no violation of the lemon law statute.

The trial court concluded that the statute did in fact require the consumer to specify the remedy selected. The statute provides "at the direction of a consumer" in regard to whether the manufacturer or dealer is to either accept return of the old vehicle and replace it with a comparable new vehicle or refund the purchase price.

The court found the phrase "at the direction of a consumer" to be unambiguous—*it required the consumer to make a choice and communicate that choice to the manufacturer* or dealer. Because the consumer failed to specify whether they wanted a new vehicle or a refund of the purchase price, the consumer's notice under the lemon law was defective.

The consumer argued that there was no statutory prohibition against a consumer asking for *either* a replacement vehicle or, alternatively, a refund. The consumer urged the court that if the consumer had no preference as to either of the two forms of relief, a consumer should be allowed to present both options to the manufacturer. The courts rejected that argument because it was contrary to the clear language of the statute.

The lemon law, said the court in *Berends*, provided the consumer with a powerful tool, but it also imposed on the consumer the responsibility of electing a specific remedy. Caveat emptor.

Tom Berends purchased a new Mack truck on May 28, 1999, and he immediately began to have serious mechanical issues with the vehicle.

Berends took the problematic truck to the dealership in Eau Claire, Wisconsin, and to an authorized facility in Las Vegas, Nevada, at least seven times for the same issue. Before Berends knew it, the truck was out of service for more than 30 days.

About four and a half months after its purchase—in early October—Berends notified the dealership that the Mack truck was a lemon under state law. On October 14, Berends's attorney provided the Mack truck company with the required notice, which stated:

> Under the provisions of the lemon law, this is a written demand for relief as outlined in that law.
>
> At this time, Mr. Berends is still having the same warranty problems with his vehicle. These defects have substantially impaired the use, safety and market value of his vehicle. Mr. Berends, therefore, demands that you *either repair these defects* within seven business days, accept the return of his vehicle and within 30 days of the return, *provide him with a vehicle acceptable to*

> *him, or provide him with a refund* calculated within accordance of the Lemon Law.
>
> Failure to comply with the Lemon Law is a violation of the statute and you may be subject to double damages, as well as attorney's fees and court costs if this matter is taken to court. (Emphasis added)

On November 26, Berends filed suit, alleging that the Mack Truck Company had violated the lemon law by failing to accept return of his vehicle and replace it with a comparable new vehicle. Berends sought to recover the full purchase price of the truck, double damages, and attorney fees.

Mack Truck denied the allegations and alleged as an affirmative defense that Berends's notice was defective because:

- It failed to specify whether a refund or vehicle replacement was requested, and
- It failed to indicate Berends's willingness to transfer title to Mack Truck.

The trial court concluded that the letter indeed *did* in fact fail to satisfy the requirements of the lemon law statute, and as a result, the court granted judgment in Mack Truck's favor. Berends appealed.

The appellate court noted that the lemon law was a remedial statute designed to rectify the problem of a new automotive buyer faced with a lemon. The statute provided that:

- If a new motor vehicle did not conform to an express warranty,
- The consumer reported the nonconformity, and
- The consumer made the vehicle available for repair before either the expiration of the warranty or one year after delivery of the vehicle, the nonconformity had to be repaired.

If the nonconformity was not repaired, the consumer's remedies under the lemon law statute included the following:

> If after a *reasonable attempt to repair the nonconformity* is not repaired, the manufacturer shall carry out the requirement [below], whichever is appropriate. . . .

2. *At the direction of a consumer described* [above], do one of the following:
   a. Accept return of the motor vehicle and *replace the motor vehicle with a comparable new motor vehicle* and refund any collateral costs.
   b. Accept return of the motor vehicle and *refund to the consumer* and to any holder of a perfected security interest in the consumer's motor vehicle, as their interest may appear, the full purchase price plus any sales tax, finance charge, amount paid by the consumer at the point of sale and collateral costs, less a reasonable allowance for use. . . .
   c. To receive a comparable new motor vehicle or a refund due a consumer shall offer to the manufacturer of the motor vehicle having the nonconformity to *transfer title of that motor vehicle to that manufacturer*. No later than 30 days after that offer, the manufacturer shall provide the consumer with the comparable new motor vehicle or refund. (Emphasis added)

If the manufacturer failed to provide the consumer's specified remedy, the consumer could then bring a lawsuit to recover damages caused by the violation.

In other words, it was the *manufacturer's* failure to comply with a proper notice that gave rise to a violation of the statute and triggered the consumer's right to remedies. If the consumer prevailed in litigation, the court was instructed to award "twice the amount of any pecuniary loss, together with costs, disbursements and reasonable attorney fees, and any equitable relief the court determines appropriate."

Berends's action was premised on his allegation that Mack Truck failed to provide him with a comparable new motor vehicle. Mack Truck argued that because Berends's notice was defective, there was no violation of the lemon law statute.

The trial court concluded that the statute did in fact require the consumer to *specify* the remedy selected. The statute provided, "At the direction of a consumer," as regards whether the manufacturer was to accept return of the old vehicle and replace it with a comparable new vehicle or refund the purchase price.

The court found that the phrase "at the direction of a consumer" was unambiguous—it *required* the consumer to make a choice and communicate that choice to the manufacturer. Because Berends failed to specify whether he wanted a new vehicle or a refund of the purchase price, his notice under the lemon law was defective.

Berends argued that there was no statutory prohibition against a consumer asking for either a replacement vehicle or, alternatively, a refund. He urged the court: "If the consumer has no preference as to either of the two forms of relief, a consumer should be allowed to present both options to the manufacturer." Berends contended that allowing a consumer to accept either remedy provided a wider range of options and made resolution of the dispute more likely.

The court rejected Berends's argument because it was contrary to the plain language of the statute. The lemon law clearly provided that the manufacturer "shall carry out the requirement" and that "At the direction of a consumer, the manufacturer do one of the following. . . ."

Under the statute, the manufacturer was provided no choice. The lemon law provided the consumer with a powerful tool, but it also imposed on the consumer the responsibility of electing a specific remedy. Only the legislature, not the courts, had the power to specify otherwise.

Berends's suggestion, said the court, that he would be satisfied if Mack Truck repaired the vehicle within seven days was inconsistent with giving the manufacturer notice under the lemon law.

The lemon law statute required the manufacturer to provide the consumer with a new vehicle or refund of the purchase price within 30 days of the consumer's request. By providing Mack Truck with a *third* option, Berends failed to follow the clear language of the statute, and as a result, Berends rendered his notice defective.

Berends also argued that his notice was proper because it conformed with a form letter distributed by the Department of Transportation (DOT) to consumers seeking assistance with lemon law claims. The DOT letter suggested the following language: "I, therefore, demand that you either repair these defects within seven business days or that you accept the return of my car and within thirty (30) days of the return provide me with a vehicle acceptable to me or a refund calculated in accordance with the Lemon Law."

The obvious problem with this language, the court pointed out, was that it failed to specify which remedy the consumer was electing and that it proposed a third remedy. The court expressed its sympathy with a consumer who unknowingly used a DOT form that was not in accordance with the statutory requirements, but the court would not agree to permit such a form as proper notice.

Berends no doubt knew that the DOT had no legal authority to promulgate forms, but he argued that a consumer should not be penalized for using a form that did not directly conflict with the lemon law. Berends offered no legal authority for this proposition.

Berends argued that even if his notice was deficient, Mack Truck's omission in responding to the notice within 30 days produced a result contrary to the intent of the law. The court held that even if this allegation was true, it did not negate Berends's duties under the law.

The court reasoned that, given the significant penalties imposed upon a manufacturer for failure to provide a remedy within 30 days, it was only fair to require consumers to follow the statute.

The summary judgment in favor of Mack Truck would therefore stand, and Mr. Berends's next lemon law notice would no doubt be a little more *precise.*

5

Release Requirement

Practice Pointer

The manufacturer or dealer of a vehicle deemed to be a *lemon cannot require the consumer to sign a general release before satisfying the refund remedy provisions of the lemon law*. Most statutes expressly provide that the lemon law "does not limit rights or remedies available to a consumer under any other law." Any nonlemon law claims related to a faulty vehicle must be pled separately.

In the case that follows—*Chariton v. Saturn Corp.*, 238 Wis.2d 27 (2000)—rather than acknowledge that the manufacturer had fulfilled its obligations under the lemon law, the manufacturer's release barred all suits having to do with the car. The lemon law prohibits a manufacturer or dealer from requiring the consumer to sign such a release.

And, just as a dispute about the amount of a refund does not toll the period in which the manufacturer or dealer must meet the consumer's complaint, the reluctance of the consumer to sign the manufacturer's release does not suspend the deadline. Regardless of the status of negotiations between the manufacturer and consumer, the lemon law requires the manufacturer to provide a refund within the time required by the statute.

Barbara Chariton bought a new 1996 Saturn at a Wisconsin dealership, and there was no question in anyone's mind that the car was a lemon.

Pursuant to Saturn's informal dispute settlement procedure, Chariton submitted a customer claim form to the Better Business Bureau Auto Line. About a week later, Chariton notified Saturn that she wanted to transfer the vehicle's title and receive a refund for the car under the lemon law.

In response, Saturn offered Chariton a total refund of $20,170.75. Saturn's letter required Chariton to sign a general settlement and release that stated:

> *By accepting this offer Ms. Chariton agrees to complete all necessary documents* to transfer title of the vehicle to Saturn Corporation including but not limited to a power of attorney (to correct any errors in title), an odometer statement *and a General Settlement Agreement and Release.* (Emphasis added)

Chariton responded that the total refund should be $176.72 more than Saturn offered—in other words, a total of $20,347.47—and that Chariton would "not necessarily sign whatever materials that you propose, if the same are not required by the Lemon Law." Chariton did not sign the general settlement and release proposed by Saturn.

Ultimately, the 30 days in which Saturn was required to tender the refund expired, and Chariton filed suit, claiming a violation of the lemon law. Saturn moved for summary judgment, arguing that Chariton's claim should be dismissed because Saturn had made an offer within the 30-day period and that Chariton's "failure to participate in the exchange should not work to create liability for Saturn."

After the trial court denied Saturn's motion, the parties stipulated to an entry of judgment in favor of Chariton for $38,874.69—which consisted of $22,374.69 in pecuniary damages and $16,500 for attorney's fees and other costs recoverable under the law.

On appeal, Saturn argued that the lemon law did not specifically prohibit it from requiring the consumer to sign a general settlement and release as part of the manufacturer's refund. Chariton claimed, on the other hand, that a manufacturer could not require a consumer to sign such a release before issuing a refund under the lemon law.

After a review of the statute, the appellate court agreed that the statute did *not* contemplate requiring the consumer sign a general release in order to obtain a refund. The statute expressly stated that the lemon law "does not limit rights or remedies available to a consumer under any other law."

A survey of the case law made it clear that any non-lemon law claims related to a faulty vehicle must be pled separately. Rather than acknowledge that Saturn had fulfilled its obligations under the lemon law, Saturn's release would have barred *any* suit against *anyone* about *anything* having to do with the car. The statute, the court held, prohibited a consumer from being required to sign such a release.

Furthermore, just as a dispute about the amount of refund did not toll the 30-day period, Chariton's reluctance to sign Saturn's release did not suspend the deadline in this case. Regardless of the status of negotiations, the lemon law required that the manufacturer provide a refund within 30 days.

In other words, there were no excuses for the manufacturer's failure to comply with the strict requirements of the lemon law statute—no matter how seemingly harsh the consequences.

6

Title Details

PRACTICE POINTER

Lemon laws place *certain duties on consumers who seek its statutory remedies, including the obligation to deliver the vehicle and the title* to the manufacturer *before obtaining a replacement vehicle or refund.* If the consumer does not meet these requirements, the manufacturer is *not* required to provide the remedies set forth in the statute. The legislature intends that these mutual obligations be performed as a *quid pro quo* which occurs more or less concurrently.

This concurrent scenario did not occur in the case that follows—*Smyser v. Western Star Trucks Corp.*, 634 N.W.2d 134 (Wisc. 2001)—because many months before the consumer made a claim under the lemon law, the consumer surrendered possession of the vehicle to the dealer, who sold it to a third party.

According to the court, there is no presumption that the legislature intended to resolve all difficult lemon law questions in favor of liability. A court upsets the remedial scheme if it pushes the statute more in favor of the consumer than its plain language allows.

Charles Smyser purchased a new truck from Racine Truck, an authorized Wisconsin dealership for the Western Star line of trucks, on January 31, 1997.

The purchase price for the truck was $86,496.39, and Smyser financed $82,962.42 of that amount through Orix Credit Alliance, Inc., which, as the lienholder, retained possession of the vehicle's title.

Almost immediately, Smyser experienced severe vibration problems with the truck. Smyser attempted to have the vehicle repaired at various Western Star dealers, including Racine Truck, but the issue persisted. Western Star conceded that there was a warranty nonconformity and agreed that the vehicle was a lemon under the statute.

About a year and a half after the truck's purchase—on June 19, 1998—Smyser informed Western Star that he was not going to make any further loan payments. Smyser also advised Orix, the lender, of this fact, and Orix told Smyser to surrender the vehicle to Racine Truck.

Smyser spoke with Racine Truck's manager, who agreed to accept the return of the vehicle. A few days later, Smyser left the truck at the dealership, and Smyser signed a power of attorney authorizing Racine Truck to transfer his interest in the vehicle. Racine Truck obtained clear title by paying Orix the sum of $65,000, the amount of Smyser's loan balance. A few days later, Racine Truck sold the vehicle to a third party.

Some 10 months later, Smyser wrote to Western Star seeking monetary relief under the lemon law in the amount of $41,019.26. Because of Smyser's tardy demand, Western Star rejected the claim.

Smyser then filed suit against Western Star and Racine Truck alleging, among other things, a violation of the lemon law.

Western Star and Racine Truck moved for summary judgment. The trial court determined that Western Star had made a reasonable attempt to repair the vehicle, but that the nonconformity had not been remedied.

However, because Smyser had previously surrendered the vehicle and title to Racine Truck and the vehicle had been sold to a third party, the court concluded that Smyser was *not* a consumer as defined under the lemon law and therefore could not obtain statutory relief.

On appeal, Smyser asserted that the lemon law obligated a manufacturer to repair a nonconformity covered by a warranty and that if that nonconformity was not fixed, the consumer could either obtain a replacement vehicle or a refund and related costs.

In order to receive a replacement vehicle or refund, the statute specifically required the consumer to first make an offer to transfer the vehicle's title back to the manufacturer. In other words, when the manufacturer provided the replacement vehicle or refund, the consumer had to deliver the vehicle and its title to the manufacturer.

It was clear that at the time he made his lemon law claim, Smyser could *not* have satisfied these requirements because he had already surrendered the vehicle and title to Racine Truck.

Unfortunately, Smyser did not take the actions required by the lemon law regarding the title of the vehicle. In fact, Smyser did not even raise the possibility of a lemon law claim until some 10 months after Smyser had returned the truck—long after Racine Truck had sold the vehicle to a third party.

Smyser argued that it made no difference that he surrendered the vehicle and its title before he made his demand for a refund. He argued that the lemon law was a remedial statute that should be liberally construed to protect consumers from warranty abuses by manufacturers.

The court responded that in spite of the lemon law's clearly stated remedial purpose, the statute nonetheless placed certain duties on consumers who sought its remedies. Among these duties was the obligation of the consumer to deliver the vehicle and title to the manufacturer.

These consumer obligations were stated in clear and unambiguous terms, particularly as to the timing of the return delivery of the vehicle and the title. The statute reads as follows:

> When the manufacturer provides the new motor vehicle or refund, the consumer shall *return the motor vehicle and provide the certificate of title*. (Emphasis added)

The court pointed out that the legislature intended that these mutual obligations be performed as a *quid pro quo* which would occur more or less concurrently. This scenario did not occur in the present case because—10 months before he had made any claim under the lemon law—Smyser had surrendered his possession and interest in the vehicle to Racine Truck, which sold it to a third party.

There was no presumption, the court explained, that when a legislature concerned itself with some abuse—such as the sale of defective automobiles—that it meant to resolve *all* difficult questions in favor of liability. Remedial statutes, like all other statutes, are compromises, and a court would upset the balance if it pushed the statute closer to the victim side of the line than the language of the statute allowed.

In other words, Smyser would have the court rewrite the clear and unambiguous terms of the lemon law simply because the statute was a remedial measure in favor of consumers. The court refused to go that far.

Smyser had simply failed to follow the letter of the statutory language, and as a result, his desperate plea for a lemon law remedy fell on deaf ears.

7

Classes of Consumer

PRACTICE POINTER

Most lemon laws define "consumer" to include "a purchaser or lessee" of a new motor *vehicle that is used for "personal, family, or household purposes"* a specified percentage of the time.

In the case that follows—*Green v. BMW of North America, LLC*, 2011 WL 6306657 (Minn. 2011)—the manufacturer argues that the consumer was not a consumer because she did not personally use the vehicle at least 40 percent of the time and that her son's usage cannot constitute her "family" use.

By its terms, the lemon law usage requirement modifies the term *vehicle*, not the phrase "purchaser or lessee," and therefore *does not limit who may drive the vehicle, as long as that usage is for one of the specified purposes.* The manufacturer's focus on actual usage by the purchaser or lessee would exclude numerous purchasers and lessees simply because they permitted others the use of their vehicles.

A lessee is considered a consumer if the leased vehicle is used at least 40 percent of the time for personal, family, or household purposes. Even if the lemon law does not define "family," the term is generally considered to include, at a minimum, parents and children.

On May 31, 2007, Marie Green signed a 39-month lease for a new 2007 BMW 328xi. Green paid $5,000 initially and then agreed to make monthly payments of $591.58, for a total sum of $27,803.04.

Although Green was the sole lessee who made all of the lease payments, she rarely drove the vehicle, and after the first year she did not drive it at all. Instead, she gave exclusive use of the car to her adult son, Michael McDonough.

Over the course of the lease term, McDonough brought the vehicle to various BMW authorized dealerships for service least 16 times, with two recurring problems:

- An intermittently hesitating in acceleration from a stop or while driving in traffic, and
- A malfunctioning sunroof.

McDonough first brought the vehicle in for service in September 2007 because of the acceleration problem. McDonough explained that the vehicle sometimes lagged for several seconds after he depressed the accelerator. The problem was most pronounced when moving from a stationary position, but it also occurred when maneuvering through traffic.

McDonough returned the car for the same problem in February and June 2008. The dealership assured McDonough that the vehicle was operating properly.

Meanwhile, McDonough continued to experience the issue, and he brought the car to the second dealership for that problem in February 2009. The service personnel submitted a written request to BMW to investigate the complaint further but did not perform any repairs.

McDonough also complained that the sunroof was rattling in June 2008, and again the following month. In August 2008, McDonough took the car to a second BMW authorized dealership complaining about the same problem. After an unsuccessful attempt to repair the sunroof, the dealership replaced the sunroof cassette.

McDonough returned to the dealership in May 2009, complaining that the new sunroof occasionally opened on its own when he was trying to close it. The dealership told McDonough that it could not duplicate the problem and returned the vehicle to McDonough without making any repairs. McDonough returned to the dealership with the same sunroof complaint in August 2009, and again, the dealership performed no repairs.

As the lessor of the BMW, Green filed suit for lemon law and warranty claims. After a four-day bench trial, the district court found in favor of Green on all claims related to the acceleration hesitation and sunroof problems. The trial court ordered BMW to refund Green the lease price, as well as the astounding sum of $221,499.50 for attorney fees and $7,565.40 for litigation costs.

On BMW's appeal, the appellate court held that the trial court did not err in concluding that Green was a "consumer" within the meaning of the lemon law.

The lemon law defines "consumer" in two parts:

- A person claiming the law's protection must be a purchaser or lessee of a new motor vehicle, and
- The vehicle must be "used for personal, family, or household purposes at least 40 percent of the time."

The statute defined "consumer" as "the purchaser or lessee, other than for purposes of resale or sublease, of a new motor vehicle used for personal, family, or household purposes at least 40 percent of the time." BMW argued that Green was not a consumer because she did not personally use the vehicle at least 40 percent of the time and her son's usage did not constitute her "family" use.

Whether Green was a "consumer" based on the undisputed facts regarding the vehicle's use presented to the court a question of statutory interpretation and the construction of words and phrases according to their plain and ordinary meaning.

BMW contended that, although Green leased the vehicle, she was not a consumer because she did not actually drive the vehicle. The court disagreed. By its terms, the usage requirement plainly modified the term *vehicle,* not the phrase "purchaser or lessee," and therefore did not limit *who* could drive the vehicle, as long as that usage was one of the specified purposes.

Not only did BMW's focus on actual usage by the purchaser or lessee run counter to the plain language of the statute, but it would lead to almost absurd results by excluding numerous purchasers and lessees simply because they permitted others the use of their vehicles.

The court did agree with BMW's argument that the usage requirement, as an element of the statutory definition of the term *consumer,* was tethered to the purchaser or lessee. While the statute did not expressly limit who could drive the vehicle, the "personal, family, or household purposes" reference was plainly those of the purchaser or lessee. Thus, Green would be considered a consumer if the vehicle she leased was used at least 40 percent of the time for her personal, family, or household purposes.

BMW argued that even if the language of the usage requirement itself was broad enough to encompass usage by those other than the purchaser or lessee, such an interpretation was contrary to provisions that permitted a manufacturer to subtract "a reasonable allowance for the consumer's use of the vehicle" from the amount to be refunded for the purchase or lease price of an automobile considered to be a lemon.

BMW claimed that use could not be "the consumer's use" or "directly attributable to use by the consumer" unless the consumer actually drove the vehicle. The court was not persuaded by this argument.

As for the issue of whether McDonough's use of the vehicle constituted use for Green's "personal, family, or household purposes," the court noted that the lemon law did not define "family," but that a family is generally considered to include, at a minimum, parents and children.

BMW asserted that McDonough did not fall within the family category because he was an adult and no longer resided in Green's household as her dependent.

The court held that although family and household were considered equivalent in some circumstances, the legislature plainly distinguished between the two in the lemon law by separating the terms with the disjunctive "or." The definition of "family" might overlap with, but could not be subsumed by, the term *household*, as BMW argued.

The plain meaning of the term *family* included McDonough, and the fact that he no longer resided in Green's household did not preclude consideration of his use of the car in evaluating the lemon law claim.

BMW also challenged the trial court's finding that Green's vehicle exhibited acceleration and sunroof defects that substantially impaired the use or market value of the vehicle.

As for the acceleration hesitation, the trial court heard direct testimony from four witnesses—Green, McDonough, a friend of McDonough, and a non-BMW mechanic—who drove the vehicle and experienced hesitation when trying to accelerate. These witnesses described the condition, how they responded to the condition, and how frequently the condition occurred.

The trial court also considered several BMW documents as evidence that BMW verified the acceleration hesitation but did not repair it. BMW argued that the trial court erred in relying on these documents and that without that evidence the record did not support a finding that the vehicle had an acceleration hesitation.

The appellate court held that the trial court's finding that the vehicle hesitated on acceleration found support in the documents from BMW and the testimony of the four witnesses who personally experienced the condition. In particular, the investigation initiated by the second dealership supported the finding that the dealership—and therefore BMW—verified the acceleration hesitation.

BMW also contended that any acceleration hesitation was not a defect requiring repair, but rather a normal part of how the vehicle operates in "economy" (or automatic mode), as demonstrated by the fact that the hesitation did not occur when the vehicle was driven in "sport" (or manual mode).

The great weight of the evidence, the court asserted, indicated otherwise. While at least one witness for BMW testified that some hesitation was to be expected when the vehicle operated in the default economy mode, almost all of the evidence indicated that the condition was a problem.

This condition was particularly apparent in the records from the second dealership because, as the trial court found, it was "highly unlikely that upon finding nothing wrong with the vehicle's acceleration, the technician would take what he himself described as a search for 'corrective action' by engaging BMW's engineers to resolve a nonexistent problem." The court concluded that the trial court did not err by finding that the vehicle's acceleration hesitation was a defect.

Having found that the acceleration hesitation constituted a defect, the court turned to the trial court's finding that it impaired the vehicle's use or market value. The record revealed sufficient support for that finding.

Green and McDonough testified that the acceleration hesitation occurred often ("intermittently" and "on a daily basis") and affected the vehicle's operation. Green testified that she felt unsafe in the vehicle because of the hesitation and refused to drive it after the first year of the lease. McDonough said that he continued to drive the vehicle but felt unsafe because the vehicle was "seriously unreliable in acceleration." He explained that the acceleration hesitation prevented him from pulling out in traffic as he normally would because he was unsure if the vehicle would hesitate and leave him vulnerable to a collision.

BMW asserted, on the other hand, that there was not substantial impairment of the vehicle's use as shown by the car's high mileage, which demonstrated that the hesitation did not interfere with McDonogh's frequent use of the vehicle.

The court held that while high mileage on a vehicle could support a finding that a defect did not substantially impair the vehicle's usage, the mileage did not necessarily undermine a finding that a defect substantially impaired the vehicle's use. The lemon law statute did not require *total* impairment of the vehicle's use or value.

The fact that McDonough continued to drive a vehicle that he considered unsafe—and that others, including Green, refused to drive—was not determinative of substantial impairment, the court said. Green presented significant evidence that the vehicle exhibited an intermittent but recurring hesitation in acceleration, that the hesitation generally lasted for several seconds or more, and that the problem occurred both from a stop and as the vehicle was maneuvered in traffic.

The appellate court concluded that the trial court's finding that the acceleration hesitation substantially impaired the use of the vehicle was therefore not clearly erroneous.

BMW primarily challenged the trial court's finding that BMW breached its warranties to Green by failing to repair defects in the vehicle within a reasonable time. The appellate court's finding that the trial court did not clearly err in finding that the vehicle had an acceleration defect that substantially impaired its use and that BMW failed to correct the issue after reasonable opportunity to do so established facts showing a breach of BMW's warranties.

BMW also argued that the trial court erred in finding that Green established damages. BMW argued that Green failed to prove the difference between "the value of the goods accepted and the value they would have had if they had been as warranted" because she did not provide evidence of the value of the vehicle in its defective condition. The court disagreed.

The trial court found that the sunroof replacement, which failed to make the sunroof function properly, cost $1,323.38, and that diagnosis and repair of the acceleration defect would cost $2,500 to $3,000. The court concluded that those findings supported the trial court's determination that Green successfully proved a diminution in the value of the vehicle.

Consumers who prevailed under the lemon law were entitled to "recover costs and disbursements, including reasonable attorney's fees incurred in the civil action." The appellate court reviewed the trial court's grant of attorney fees for an abuse of discretion.

BMW argued that the district court abused its discretion by awarding Green almost all of her requested fees, challenging the reasonableness of the hours expended by Green's counsel, the reasonableness of the hourly rate, and the trial court's refusal to consider the value of the underlying claim in awarding attorney fees.

BMW first challenged the reasonableness of the hours expended. Billing records submitted by Green's counsel detail two years' work on Green's case, totaling about 600 attorney hours (between two attorneys) and about 10 paralegal hours. Green also offered the affidavits of her attorneys, supporting affidavits from two other local experienced consumer-rights attorneys, and numerous fee orders from other consumer-rights cases.

BMW argued that the hours expended were excessive and particularly criticized the amount of time spent on preparation and review of proposed findings of fact. The trial court disagreed, finding that the time spent on this matter by Green's counsel and paralegal was reasonable and necessary, particularly after BMW "vigorously defended" the case.

The appellate court commented that the number of hours counsel spent on this case was high, but it recognized that a significant amount of time was necessary to meet the unique demands of a bench trial. By awarding fees in an amount greater than cases involving settlement or jury trials, the trial court did not, as BMW asserted, "merely accept at face value the 'hours expended'" by Green's attorneys but recognized the unique circumstances of this case. The appellate court concluded that the trial court did not clearly err in finding the hours billed were reasonable and necessary to establish Green's claims.

BMW next argued that the district court clearly erred in accepting the $350 and $375 hourly rates billed by Green's attorneys. The trial court considered the experience of the attorneys, the affidavit testimony of other attorneys in the community as to a reasonable hourly rate for the work performed, and attorney-fee orders in other consumer-rights cases, all of which indicated attorney fees of $350 to $375 were within the range of market rates. Because the record supported the trial court's determination that Green's counsels' hourly rates were reasonable, the appellate court discerned no clear error.

Finally, BMW argued that the district court erred by refusing to consider the extent of the attorney fees in relation to the "amount involved"—the approximately $27,000 that Green stood to recover. The appellate held that a trial court should not consider the amount involved in the litigation when awarding attorney fees. Such an approach would undermine the purpose of the fee-shifting provision, which recognized that the amount involved may be minimal compared with the effort required to succeed on the claim.

The appellate court concluded that the trial court did not abuse its discretion by declining to reduce the attorney's fees solely because the amount in controversy was relatively small.

In the end, BMW was painfully stuck not only with a lemon produced by its assembly line, but also with a hefty bill from the lawyers on the other side.

8

Business Use

PRACTICE POINTER

Lemon laws are intended to provide protection for individual, nonbusiness consumers, and evidence that the *vehicle is purchased by a business or used for business purposes removes it from the protection of the statute*. The statutes generally require the court to initially look at the use of the vehicle and then at the person who was driving it.

Above all, lemon laws are intended to assist consumers who need the most help—those who normally used their vehicles for "personal, family, or household purposes"—and not just for any person or business that happened to be privy to a contract to enforce the obligations of the warranty.

In the case that follows—*Jones v. General Motors Corporation*, 953 P.2d 1104 (N.M. 1998)—there was evidence that the consumer bought the car through his company, used the car to a significant extent for business purposes, listed the vehicle as an asset of his company, and depreciated it on the company's tax returns.

On June 24, 1993, Earl Jones purchased in the name of his business, Chaveroo Supply Company, a brand-new Cadillac Eldorado from a dealership in Hobbs, New Mexico, for the sum of $37,979.36.

From June 1993 to March 1994, the Eldorado required numerous repairs, and it was out of service for at least 28 days. Jones notified both the dealer and General Motors Corporation of the problems with the car, and while the dealership was afforded numerous opportunities to repair the defects, it was only partially successful.

Jones sued GMC for damages under the lemon law. At trial, Jones testified that he purchased the Cadillac for his personal use, but there was evidence that Jones bought the car through his company and used the car to a significant extent for business purposes, namely:

- The car was listed as an asset of Chaveroo Supply Co. (Jones's wholly owned oil field supply business) and was depreciated on Chaveroo's tax returns.
- The business paid for the Cadillac and some of its repairs, and Jones admitted he used the car to visit offices relating to his business.
- The car showed extensive mileage in a short period of time (64,716 miles in 27 months) and over rough roads while engaged in the oil field supply business.

Although the trial court initially found that Jones used the car for nonbusiness purposes 95 percent of the time, the court amended that finding and concluded that the car "was owned by Chaveroo Supply Company, Inc. and was furnished to the Plaintiff Earl Jones for both business and personal use." In the end, the trial court dismissed Jones's lemon law claim, concluding that Jones was not a consumer as defined under the statute.

Jones raised three points on appeal: (1) whether the trial court erred in finding Jones was not a consumer for purposes of the lemon law, (2) whether the trial court erred in determining that Jones could not recover under the lemon law, and (3) whether the trial court erred by amending its finding of fact concerning Jones's personal and business use of the car.

The court, first of all, noted the general purpose of the lemon law: to afford protection to consumers who bought new cars that turned out to be defective. The statute required that if a manufacturer could not repair the car to conform to its express warranties, then the consumer was entitled to either a replacement vehicle or a refund of the full purchase price (which was the remedy that Jones sought).

However, the scope of the lemon law was limited, and its protection extended only to "consumers." The dispute in this case centered on whether Jones was a consumer.

The lemon law statute defined "consumer" as follows:

> The purchaser, other than for purposes of resale, of a new motor vehicle *normally used for personal, family, or household purposes*, any person to whom such a motor *vehicle has been transferred* during the duration of an express warranty applicable to the motor vehicle and any other person entitled by the terms of the warranty to *enforce the obligations of the warranty*. [Emphasis added]

Jones claimed that this statute envisioned three types of users, any one of which would qualify him as a consumer:

- The purchaser of the vehicle,
- Anyone to whom the vehicle was transferred during the terms of the warranty, or
- Anyone else entitled to enforce the obligations of the warranty.

Jones argued that he was a consumer for the purposes of the statute because he was unquestionably a person entitled "to enforce the obligations of the warranty."

The court disagreed with Jones's interpretation of the law. The statute limited protection to persons whose vehicles were "normally used for personal, family, or household purposes." Whether a purchaser of a vehicle was a consumer for the purposes of the lemon law required a two-part analysis. The statute first defined consumers by their use of their vehicles. If the vehicle was normally used for personal, family, or household reasons, the statute then laid out the three categories of users who qualified as consumers.

As a result, the statute required the court to first look at the use of the vehicle and second at the person who was using it. Under this analysis, the trial court reasonably concluded, based on substantial evidence, that Jones was *not* a consumer. The car was not shown to have been "normally used for personal, family, or household purposes."

The court, then, did not need to proceed to the second part of the analysis (determining the class of user); therefore it was immaterial that Jones was a "person entitled by the terms of the warranty to enforce the obligations of the warranty."

The lemon law contained no specific language specifically addressing its purpose, but an intent "to improve consumer remedies" was strongly indicated in the statute, and various provisions of the law made it abundantly clear that its protections applied to consumers only.

The court was not persuaded that the three parts of the definition of "consumer" were meant to be independent of the vehicle's use. The three-part definition of consumer was contained entirely within one sentence and each part was not separately enumerated.

The third part of the definition, read alone, stated that a consumer was "any other person entitled by the terms of the warranty to enforce the obligations of the warranty," but the word "warranty" referred back to the "express warranty applicable to the motor vehicle" defined in the second part, which in turn referred back to "the new motor vehicle normally used for personal, family, or household purposes" defined in the first part.

The provision, then, referred to one integrated definition of consumer. The sentence provided no reference for "the warranty" other than "an express warranty applicable to the motor vehicle normally used for personal, family, or household purposes."

Unless the definition of motor vehicle in the first part of the statute was applied to the third, the third part was too vague to be meaningful and would extend the coverage of the statute far beyond the most widely accepted purpose of lemon laws, which was to provide protection for individual, nonbusiness consumers, most of whom regard a new automobile as the single largest consumer purchase, in dollars, other than the purchase of a house.

The court explained that the legislature created the remedies for purchasers who needed the most help—those who normally used their vehicles for "personal, family, or household purposes"—and not just for any person or business that happened to be privy to a contract to enforce the obligations of the warranty. The court's determination of legislative purpose was thus supported by the language of the statute.

The trial court's conclusion that Jones was not a consumer, then, was supported by substantial evidence that his beloved Eldorado was, in fact, a company car.

9

Lengthy Repair Time

PRACTICE POINTER

Unavailability of a new car is a key element of the lemon law. *The fact that a consumer cannot drive a newly purchased vehicle for a full month in the first year of ownership automatically defines the vehicle as a lemon in most states.*

The statute does not create a "presumption" of recovery, but rather "a presumption that a reasonable number of attempts to conform the vehicle to warranty have been made." The statute studiously avoids leaving the term *reasonableness* open to interpretation, and instead defines what is reasonable in strict terms.

In other words, the "enough is enough" portion of the statute is a type of statute of limitations: it establishes in well-defined terms the limit of frustration a consumer has to endure. The statute, in effect, clarifies the cutoff point for reasonableness.

In the case that follows—*Royster v. Toyota Motor Sales, U.S.A., Inc.*, 759 N.E.2d 531 (Ohio 2991)—a manufacturer under the statute has three attempts to repair a particular nonconformity, eight attempts to repair any combination of nonconformities, and one attempt to repair a nonconformity that results in a condition that renders the vehicle extremely dangerous to drive.

The lemon law recognizes that if problems persist or cannot be repaired in a specified period of time, then the consumer is presumed to have *not* received what was bargained for.

On February 3, 1996, Kimberly Royster leased a new Toyota 4–Runner at a dealership in Cleveland Heights, Ohio. The SUV was warranted by Toyota and included a three-year/30,000-mile warranty.

About nine months later, with an odometer reading of about 10,000 miles, Royster noticed that the 4-Runner was leaking an ominous red fluid, and the vehicle was promptly towed to the dealership.

The dealership determined that the 4-Runner had a faulty head gasket, but the dealership encountered troubles locating the correct part and it was unable to complete the repair until December 31—after the vehicle had been unavailable to Royster for a total of 55 days. In the meantime, the dealership provided Royster with a complimentary Toyota Camry for her daily driving needs.

On January 6, 1997, Royster returned the 4-Runner to the dealership to repair the brakes. Royster experienced no further mechanical difficulties, but on May 30, she had had enough and filed a lemon lawsuit against Toyota. Both parties filed motions for summary judgment.

The trial court granted Royster's motion based on the lemon law's presumption in favor of recovery if a vehicle is "out of service by reason of repair for a cumulative total of 30 or more calendar days" in the first year of ownership. The court awarded Royster the sum of $38,565.54 in damages and another $7,649 judgment in attorney fees.

The appellate court eventually overturned the trial court's decision, holding that the trial court had erred in finding that the 55 days the car spent in the shop created a *presumption* of recovery for Royster under the lemon law.

The appellate court determined that the dealership had made a reasonable effort to repair the vehicle and was ultimately successful in conforming the car to its warranty. The court reasoned that Royster had a valid lemon law claim *only* if the vehicle had *not* conformed to its warranty after the dealership's "reasonable number of repair attempts."

The case then moved to the state supreme court, which agreed with the trial court and overruled the decision of the appellate court. The supreme court held that the lemon law was designed to protect consumers from chronically defective new automobiles by requiring manufacturers to live up to the vehicle warranties. The lemon law, the court said, provided a clear duty on the part of the manufacturer and a clear remedy to a consumer should the manufacturer breach its duty.

Under the lemon law, a vehicle manufacturer had to abide by the terms of the warranty, and if the automobile did not meet those standards, the manufacturer had to repair it (*emphasis added*):

> If a new motor vehicle *does not conform to any applicable express warranty* and the consumer reports the nonconformity to the manufacturer, its agent, or its authorized dealer during the period of one year following the date of original delivery or during the first 18,000 miles of operation, whichever is earlier, the manufacturer, its agent, or its authorized dealer shall make any *repairs as are necessary to conform the vehicle to such express warranty, notwithstanding the fact that the repairs are made after the expiration of the appropriate time period.*

The statute placed a clear duty on manufacturers, and it gave manufacturers the opportunity to make prompt repairs. The statute also provided consumers with a swift and simple remedy should the car not be made right within a reasonable number of attempts.

If repairs were unsuccessful, the statute provided remedies for consumers:

> If the manufacturer, its agent, or its authorized dealer *is unable to conform the motor vehicle to any applicable express warranty* by repairing or correcting any defect or condition that substantially impairs the use, safety, or value of the motor vehicle to the consumer after a reasonable number of repair attempts, the manufacturer shall, at the consumer's option, *replace the motor vehicle with a new motor vehicle* acceptable to the consumer *or accept return of the vehicle* from the consumer and refund each of the following:
>
> (1) The *full purchase price* including, but not limited to, charges for undercoating, transportation, and installed options;
>
> (2) All *collateral charges*, including but not limited to, sales tax, license and registration fees, and similar government charges;
>
> (3) All *finance charges* incurred by the consumer;
>
> (4) All *incidental damages*, including any reasonable fees charged by the lender for making or canceling the loan. (Emphasis added)

Thus, if a manufacturer could not repair a new automobile after a reasonable number of attempts, a consumer may request a refund or a replacement for the vehicle.

Should there be a doubt—and resulting litigation—as to what constituted "a reasonable number of repair attempts," the statute set limits:

> *It shall be presumed that a reasonable number of attempts have been undertaken* by the manufacturer, its dealer, or its authorized agent to conform a motor vehicle to any applicable express warranty if, during the period of one year following the date of original delivery or during the first 18,000 miles of operation, whichever is earlier, any of the following apply;
>
> **(A)** Substantially the same nonconformity has been *subject to repair three or more times* and continues to exist;
>
> **(B)** The vehicle is out of service by reason of repair for a cumulative total of *30 or more calendar days*;
>
> **(C)** There have been *eight or more attempts to repair* any nonconformity that substantially impairs the use and value of the motor vehicle to the consumer;
>
> **(D)** There has been at least one attempt to repair a nonconformity that results in a *condition that is likely to cause death or serious bodily injury* if the vehicle is driven, and the nonconformity continues to exist. (Emphasis added)

The appellate court held that the statute did *not* create a "presumption" of recovery, but rather "a presumption that a reasonable number of attempts to conform the vehicle to warranty have been made."

According to the appellate court, because Royster had failed to prove that the 4-Runner remained defective after Toyota's nearly two-month repair attempt, the court ruled in favor of Toyota.

In its review of the case, the state supreme court disagreed. The court explained that the lemon law recognized that occasionally new cars do have problems, but that if those problems persisted, or could not be repaired in a reasonable amount of time, then the consumer did not get what was bargained for.

In other words, the "enough is enough" portion of the statute was a type of statute of limitations—it set in well-defined terms the limit of frustration a consumer had to endure.

The statute, the supreme court noted, clarified the cutoff point for reasonableness. A manufacturer had *three* attempts to repair a particular nonconformity, *eight* attempts to correct any combination of nonconformities, and *one* attempt to repair a nonconformity that resulted in a condition that rendered the vehicle extremely dangerous to drive.

The statute avoided leaving the term *reasonableness* open to interpretation and instead defined what was reasonable in strict terms.

The provision applicable in this case marked 30 days as the limit that a consumer should have to tolerate a vehicle out of service in the first year of ownership. Whether the vehicle was drivable after those 30 days was irrelevant. Indeed, the statute spoke in terms of a cumulative 30 days out of service. Thus, the vehicle could have entered the shop on numerous occasions and could been repaired each time.

The unavailability of the new car, the court said, was the key element. The fact that a consumer could not drive a newly purchased vehicle for a full month in the first year of ownership clearly indicated that the vehicle was a lemon. The legislature arrived at 30 days as the compromise between what a consumer must endure and the time a manufacturer needed to make necessary repairs. Nothing beyond 30 days, the legislature determined, was statutorily reasonable. Once the boundaries of reasonableness were passed, the vehicle was legally classified as a lemon.

By leaving little room for interpretation, the statute was designed to avoid litigation. As a consumer protection law, the lemon law strived to be simple and consequential in order to be effective. To work well, the statute needed a stern remedy at a clearly ascertainable period of time.

For the law to take effect, the consumer only needed to prove that the automobile had been unsuccessfully repaired the requisite number of times. Unless the manufacturer could show that the defects were not substantial or were the fault of the consumer, the manufacturer was forced to replace the car or refund the purchase price.

Despite its stringent remedy, the lemon law offered protections for manufacturers. The law, for example, did not create remedies for buyers who had become disenchanted with their new vehicle for cosmetic or other trivial reasons. Instead, the vehicle's problem had to "substantially impair the use, safety, or value" of the motor vehicle to the consumer.

The lemon law also provided defenses to manufacturers. A consumer could not recover under the lemon law if the nonconformity was "the result of abuse, neglect, or the unauthorized modification or alteration of a motor vehicle by anyone other than the manufacturer, its agent, or its authorized dealer."

Still, the lemon law remained a powerful tool for consumers. The effect of the lemon law was to persuade manufacturers to be responsive when new car buyers brought their vehicles in for repair. In most cases, the threat of a remedy is enough to achieve a positive result for the parties.

The supreme court agreed with the trial court that a leaking head gasket "certainly maintains the look, feel, and potential expense of a disaster" and therefore met the statutory definition of a substantial impairment. Toyota was obviously unable to repair the problem within 30 days, and Toyota failed to assert that any of the statutory affirmative defenses were applicable.

The appellate court apparently considered the dealership's provision of a loaner car to be a *de facto* affirmative defense. The supreme court tersely disagreed with the adequacy of the loaner car remedy: "While an admirable gesture, lending a car to a consumer with a Lemon Law claim provides no statutory defense. The true focus of the Lemon Law is on the automobile. In enacting the lemon law, the legislature defined for consumers when an automobile becomes a lemon, not when a dealer is not being considerate enough."

10

Hard Deadline

Practice Pointer

Lemon law negotiations between the manufacturer and consumer of a vehicle do not delay the running of the 30-day clock for the manufacturer to issue a refund, which is typical in most states. *Once the consumer makes the offer to transfer title, the burden is on the manufacturer to comply with the 30-day requirement regardless of whether there are issues in dispute.*

When the parties cannot agree on the correct amount of the refund, the lemon law gives the manufacturer two options: pay the amount demanded by the consumer within the 30-day period, or pay the amount that the manufacturer deems appropriate within the 30-day period.

If the manufacturer pays the amount demanded by the consumer, the matter is concluded. If the manufacturer pays the amount that it deems appropriate, the consumer can take the matter to court and subject the manufacturer to possible penalties under the statute.

In the case that follows, it is clear that the rigidity of the 30-day requirement sometimes places manufacturers in a difficult position. But most courts recognize that lemon laws are policy-driven statutes aimed at leveling the playing field between consumers and manufacturers and must be strictly followed.

Mark and Anna Church purchased a new car from a Chrysler dealership in Milwaukee on July 27, 1994. Within the first year, the Churches experienced at least one warranty nonconformity with the vehicle, and the problem was never resolved by the dealer in spite of several efforts by the Churches to have it repaired.

Even Chrysler eventually agreed that the vehicle was a lemon.

Almost a year later—July 20, 1995—Anna Church wrote Chrysler and offered to transfer title to the vehicle in return for "a refund of the full purchase price" as set forth in the state's lemon law. On August 4, Chrysler indicated its intent to repurchase the vehicle by refunding the sum of $27,832.98. The company requested that the Churches accept the offer within two business days.

On August 11, the Churches informed Chrysler that the proper refund amount was in fact $30,404.82—which was $2,571.84 more than Chrysler offered—and that the Churches expected to receive that sum no later than 30 days from their initial offer on July 20 (i.e., by August 20).

On August 15, Chrysler responded, noting that the lemon law "only provides for the costs relating to the vehicle at the time of sale" and that the Churches were not entitled to reimbursement for either (1) the rebate they received at the time of purchase or (2) the cost of accessories.

Chrysler nevertheless agreed to include the price of the accessories in the refund, and Chrysler informed the Churches that they would be contacted when their checks, totaling $29,374.51, arrived at the local Chrysler office.

On August 23—33 days after Anna Church's original letter of July 20—the Churches filed suit against Chrysler alleging violation of the lemon law. On September 11, Chrysler sent the Churches two checks totaling $29,374.51.

Both parties moved for summary judgment. The trial court ruled that Chrysler had not violated the provisions of the lemon law because the parties' negotiations concerning the correct amount of the refund had delayed the 30-day deadline. The court dismissed the complaint, and the Churches appealed.

The primary issue before the appellate court was whether the lemon law set forth a *strict* 30-day time limit when the parties were in good faith negotiating the amount of the refund on the thirtieth day.

The state lemon law specifically provided that if a new motor vehicle did not conform to an express warranty, the dealership had to repair the nonconformity before the expiration of one year after delivery of the vehicle. If the nonconformity was not repaired, the dealership had to:

- Provide the consumer with a comparable new vehicle, or
- Within 30 days refund to the consumer the full purchase price plus any sales tax, finance charges, and collateral costs, less a reasonable allowance for use.

For a violation of the statute, the dealership would be liable to the consumer for *twice* the amount of any pecuniary loss, together with costs, disbursements and reasonable attorney fees, and any equitable relief the court determined appropriate.

The Churches argued that Chrysler violated the statute because it did not send them the refund checks until September 11, 1995, more than 30 days after the Churches' July 20 offer to transfer title.

Chrysler countered that the Churches' subsequent letter of August 11—in which the Churches claimed that Chrysler had miscalculated the refund—actually *removed* the refund process from the deadline of the lemon law. Alternatively, Chrysler argued that the process of negotiating the appropriate amount of refund (which began on August 11) *restarted* the 30-day time limit.

In response to Chrysler's arguments, the appellate court bluntly remarked that it was "unpersuaded."

The lemon law, reasoned the court, was "created to be a self-enforcing consumer law that provides 'important rights to motor vehicle owners.'" An important purpose of the law, said the court, was to "provide an incentive for a manufacturer to put the purchaser of a new car back to the position the purchaser thought he or she was in at the time they bought the car." The court noted that it was clear from the 30-day time limit that an additional purpose of the statute was to ensure that the manufacturer act in a timely manner.

The court rejected Chrysler's contention that the Churches' attempts to negotiate a greater refund amount removed the process from the lemon law or delayed the running of the 30-day clock. The court conceded that the Churches' letter undoubtedly complicated the process, but the language of the statute clearly required the manufacturer to issue a refund within 30 days of the consumer's offer to transfer title.

Once the consumer made the offer to transfer title, the burden was on the manufacturer to comply with the 30-day requirement regardless of whether there were items in dispute. To hold otherwise, the court said, would disturb the purpose of the statute.

When the parties could not agree on the correct amount of the refund, the lemon law gave the manufacturer two options:

- Pay the amount demanded by the consumer within the 30-day period, or
- Pay the amount that the manufacturer deemed appropriate within the 30-day period.

If the manufacturer paid the amount demanded by the consumer, the matter would be concluded. If the manufacturer paid the amount that it deemed appropriate, the consumer could take the matter to court and subject the manufacturer to the possible penalty under the lemon law.

The appellate court recognized that the rigidity of the 30-day requirement sometimes placed manufacturers in a difficult position. But the lemon law, the court explained, was a policy-driven statute aimed at leveling the playing field between consumers and manufacturers in their warranty negotiations.

If the lemon law standards proved to be too rigid or harsh, it was ultimately up to the legislature—not the courts—to resolve those requirements.

11

Difficult Buyers

PRACTICE POINTER

A consumer's duty to act in good faith while pursuing a lemon law claim is inherent in the statute itself. *Consumers fail to act in good faith when they intentionally prevent manufacturers and dealers from complying with the statute.*

In the case that follows—*Marquez v. Mercedes-Benz USA*, 751 N.W.2d 859 (Wis. 2008)—the manufacturer was ready to comply with its statutory duty but was prevented from doing so by the consumer's deliberate obstruction.

The statutory penalties of a lemon law provide an incentive for manufacturers to promptly comply with vehicle exchange and refund rules by making it costly to delay. This purpose is not served, the courts have made clear, if a consumer is allowed to inflict penalties on a manufacturer who is attempting to timely comply with the law.

Lemon laws typically give a manufacturer 30 days to meet a consumer's request for replacement or refund of a malfunctioning vehicle that cannot be repaired, and the courts have consistently refused to extend this deadline when the manufacturer and consumer cannot reach agreement on the remedy.

The courts have taken the position that the lemon law has delineated the consumer's obligations regarding efforts to repair the vehicle, and once those are met, it is the manufacturer's responsibility to refund or replace the vehicle within 30 days.

If the manufacturer does not comply, the consumer is entitled to receive harsh statutory penalties, including double damages. Many of these cases have involved a manufacturer offering an "excuse" for its inability to provide a refund within the allotted time. As one court tersely stated in an opinion concerning the manufacturer's obligations, "there are no excuses."

But what about the situation where the manufacturer was willing to pay the refund but was intentionally prevented from doing so by the consumer? Previous judicial decisions have stated that while the lemon law statute contemplated that both the manufacturer and the consumer act in good faith, the term *good faith* had never been precisely defined.

In the present case, Marco Marquez bought a new Mercedes from a Milwaukee dealership. Marquez financed the purchase with a loan from Waukesha State Bank. The car turned out to be a lemon, and on October 28, 2005, Marquez sent the Mercedes Corporation a demand for a refund. In the following days, Marquez and Mercedes had various conversations about Marquez exchanging his car for a different model and paying any price difference.

On November 23, Marquez definitively told Mercedes that he wanted a refund, *not* a replacement. Mercedes told Marquez it would contact him the Monday after the Thanksgiving weekend to arrange the details of the payment. That Monday was November 28—31 days after Mercedes received the lemon law notice.

Mercedes claimed that on the thirty-first day it called Marquez's bank about transferring the refund but that Mercedes was unable to obtain account information due to privacy laws. Mercedes then asked Marquez to contact his bank. Marquez instead called his attorney, who filed suit against Mercedes the next day. The trial court ultimately granted summary judgment to Marquez.

The state's lemon law allowed the purchaser of a new car that did not conform to its warranty to receive a comparable new vehicle or a refund after reasonable attempts to repair the car had failed. To initiate the refund process, the consumer had to first offer to transfer to the manufacturer the faulty vehicle's title. The manufacturer then had 30 days to make the refund. A manufacturer who failed to meet this deadline was subject to penalties in the form of double damages, attorney fees, costs, and other equitable relief.

Mercedes argued that it was impossible for it to make a proper refund because it did not know how much Marquez owed the bank on the auto loan and that Mercedes was required to pay the bank this amount as part of the refund. Mercedes further claimed that Marquez's failure to provide the information amounted to bad faith.

Marquez countered that Mercedes did not need the payoff amount for the loan because Mercedes could have issued a single check for the entire refund to Marquez, allowing Marquez and the bank to settle the loan between themselves.

The court acknowledged that, as a general matter, a payor could issue a multiple-party check that required the consent of all payees to cash. However, the question here was whether issuing a single check to Marquez would have placed Mercedes in compliance with the lemon law. The court concluded that it would *not.*

The bank was listed as a secured party on the title application, giving it a perfected security interest in the car. The lemon law required the manufacturer to "refund the purchase price and other costs to the consumer and to any holder of a perfected security interest in the consumer's motor vehicle, as their interest may appear."

In the court's view, the plain and ordinary meaning of the phrase "refund to any holder of a perfected security interest as its interest may appear" involved the payor transferring the *correct* sum to the secured lender—not, as Marquez suggested, giving a lump-sum check to the consumer and leaving them to sort it out with the lender.

To comply with the lemon law, Mercedes had to write a separate check to Waukesha State Bank to pay off the bank's interest in the car.

Marquez further contended that even if Mercedes needed to know the correct payoff amount to pay the refund, it already had in its possession all of the information it needed to calculate the payoff amount. Marquez pointed out that the loan document, which delineated the interest and payment terms, was attached to the lemon law notice, and therefore Mercedes only needed to use simple arithmetic to know how much to pay the bank and to pay Marquez.

The court did not agree. The loan document provided no information about Marquez's history of payments—he could have made early payments, or he could have been delinquent in the six months that passed between the purchase of the car and the delivery of the notice.

Without current information, Mercedes would have no way of knowing whether it was paying the correct amounts to Marquez and to the bank.

For this reason, the standard lemon law notice form distributed by the state Department of Transportation included a line for a consumer to provide the name of the loan provider and the loan account number, along with the statement that "by providing this information, I authorize the manufacturer to contact this financial institution for financing information needed to calculate a refund."

As Mercedes pointed out, Marquez included his lender name and loan account number with his lemon law notice, suggesting that Marquez recognized that Mercedes would need more precise loan information than it possessed. The court concluded that Mercedes did, in fact, need further payoff information to make the proper refund under the lemon law.

The court therefore had to address the second issue: If Marquez intentionally withheld this information and thereby caused Mercedes to miss the 30-day refund window, was Marquez entitled to the statutory damages for Mercedes's violation of the statute?

Previous judicial decisions were clear that negotiations between manufacturer and consumer would *not* toll the 30-day time limit of the lemon law. If the parties could not reach agreement by the thirtieth day, it was up to the manufacturer to decide whether to meet the consumer's demands or issue the refund on the terms it believed proper.

If the manufacturer took the latter course and the consumer brought a lawsuit—and the manufacturer turned out to have been wrong—the manufacturer would be required to face the statutory consequences. In any case, the manufacturer had to make payment by the thirtieth day regardless of the status of negotiations.

The court noted that this was not a case about negotiations or a manufacturer attempting to impose nonstatutory conditions for a refund. This was a case in which the manufacturer was ready to comply with its statutory duty, but was prevented from doing so by the consumer's deliberate obstruction.

There was nothing in the lemon law statute forbidding a consumer from deliberately forcing a manufacturer to violate the statute in order to reap the extra statutory damages, but the court found it unlikely that the legislature meant to allow this type of abuse.

The statutory penalties of the lemon law provided an incentive for manufacturers to promptly comply with the automobile exchange and refund rules by making it costly for the manufacturer to delay. This remedial purpose was not served, the court said, if a consumer could in essence inflict the penalties on the manufacturer even if the manufacturer was attempting to timely comply with the law.

The court reemphasized that a consumer's duty to act in good faith was inherent in the statute itself and was not imported from contract law. The court further held that a consumer failed to act in good faith when the consumer intentionally prevented the manufacturer from complying with the statute.

The court concluded that this rule was true even if, as was the case here, the manufacturer did not attempt to make a refund until near the end of the statutory time limit. Mercedes spent the bulk of the 30 days trying to induce Marquez to abandon his lemon law refund demand and accept a trade for a different auto model.

Certainly, if Mercedes had persisted in this approach beyond the 30-day window, Mercedes would be subject to the statutory damages of the lemon law. But there was nothing preventing the negotiation of alternative resolutions before the 30-day limit expired.

If Mercedes had provided Marquez with a refund on the thirtieth day, Mercedes would have been in compliance with the statute. If Mercedes stood ready to comply on the thirtieth day—and only Marquez's deliberate refusal to provide the necessary information prevented it from doing so—the court could see no reason why the fact that it was the thirtieth day should make any difference.

The court concluded that contrary conclusions could be drawn about whether Marquez was, in fact, guilty of this mischievous conduct. In particular, the differing recollections of the conversations between Marquez and Mercedes created an issue of fact, and the case was therefore remanded for trial to determine what really happened between the parties.

12

Double the Money

PRACTICE POINTER

If a court finds a violation of the lemon law, most states require it to award *double damages to the consumer, no matter how harsh the consequences to the manufacturer seem.* This is a stern warning to manufacturers dealing with warranty claims.

In the case that follows—*Hughes v. Chrysler Motors Corporation*, 542 N.W.2d 148 (Wis. 1996)—the statute required the award of double damages and reasonable attorney fees to be mandatory rather than discretionary: "The court shall award a consumer who prevails twice the amount of any pecuniary loss."

The issue then is whether the statute is intended to include the car's purchase price as pecuniary damages. The court in this case held that by including the car's purchase price as part of the pecuniary loss, the statute provides an incentive for the manufacturer to quickly resolve the matter by making delay far more costly.

John Hughes purchased a new Dodge Caravan on January 11, 1990. During his first year of ownership, Hughes took the Caravan to a dealer for transmission problems on seven separate occasions.

The repairs were ultimately unsuccessful, and Hughes retained counsel, who on June 19, 1991, demanded that Chrysler replace the car within 30 days with a "comparable new motor vehicle."

Hughes's attorney received no response within the 30 days required by the lemon law, and he contacted Chrysler again on July 29 before filing suit on August 22. On August 23, Chrysler offered to replace the vehicle without any charge, including a generous offer of a model year upgrade and no mileage charges for use of the old vehicle.

The trial court granted Hughes's motion for summary judgment and entered judgment in the amount of $74,371, which included *double* the amount Hughes paid for the Dodge Caravan, his attorney fees, and prejudgment interest.

On appeal, the first issue was whether the purchase price of the car constituted pecuniary damages within the meaning of the lemon law. Chrysler argued that a buyer's pecuniary loss was limited to the out-of-pocket expenses caused by the manufacturer's violation of the law.

Hughes contended that pecuniary loss included the purchase price of the car and that allowing the consumer to recover double the purchase price advanced the law's policies and strengthened the rights of consumers in dealing with vehicle defects under warranty.

Admittedly, the lemon law statute itself was silent as to whether pecuniary loss included the vehicle's purchase price. To determine the legislative intent behind the statute, the court examined the history of lemon laws. Prior to the enactment of lemon laws, the only types of relief available to consumers were the statutory remedies of (1) revocation of acceptance and (2) breach of warranty under the Uniform Commercial Code. Federal remedies also existed through the Magnuson–Moss Warranty Act.

These state and federal remedies, however, did not adequately protect the interests of consumers in typical defective vehicle claims. Until the enactment of lemon laws, purchasers of defective cars had no other recourse than to repeatedly bring their cars back to the shop for repairs.

The lemon law provided that if a new motor vehicle did not conform to the express warranty, the nonconformity had to be repaired before the expiration of the warranty, or one year after delivery of the vehicle, whichever occurred sooner. If the nonconformity was not repaired after reasonable attempts to repair it, the manufacturer had to accept the vehicle's return, and at the direction of the consumer, either replace the vehicle or refund to the consumer the full purchase price plus any sales tax, finance charge, and other costs, less a reasonable allowance for use.

The statute defined a reasonable attempt to repair to mean that the nonconformity was presented for repair four times and the nonconformity persisted, or that the vehicle was out of service for an aggregate of at least 30 days due to warranty nonconformities.

The lemon law was violated when the manufacturer failed to voluntarily replace or repurchase the vehicle within 30 days after receipt of the consumer's demand. This failure to voluntarily comply with the lemon law established a violation of the law and triggered its remedies.

The statute provided that:

> The court shall award a consumer who prevails in such an action *twice the amount of any pecuniary loss*, together with *costs, disbursements and reasonable attorney fees*, and any equitable relief the court determines appropriate. (Emphasis added)

The lemon law was created to be a self-enforcing consumer law that provided "important rights to motor vehicle owners." The intent behind the law was to "improve auto manufacturers' quality control and reduce the inconvenience, the expense, the frustration, the fear and the emotional trauma that lemon owners endure."

The statute was later amended to make the award of double damages and reasonable attorney fees mandatory rather than discretionary: the "court shall award a consumer who prevails twice the amount of any pecuniary loss."

Looking at the legislative history, the court concluded that the statute was intended to include the car's purchase price as pecuniary damages. Accepting Chrysler's definition of pecuniary loss, the court explained, would not significantly advance a consumer's remedies. The court reasoned that surely the lemon law was intended to do *more* than simply reiterate the remedies previously available to a consumer.

Second, by including the car's purchase price as part of the pecuniary loss, the statute provided an incentive to the manufacturer to promptly resolve the matter by making it far more costly to delay. If the only damages available were out-of-pocket costs, the statute would provide little incentive for the manufacturer to move quickly. The imposition of double damages provided the necessary motivation.

Another reason to allow double damages was to encourage manufacturers to settle legitimate warranty disputes so that consumers were not forced to litigate their cases. The manufacturer had to more carefully consider the costs of litigating the dispute when there was the prospect of paying the penalties of double damages, attorney's fees, and other costs.

Third, a potential recovery had to be large enough to give vehicle owners the incentive to bring suits against these large corporations. The threat of double damages increased the bargaining power of individual consumers.

The court noted that manufacturers not only had the resources to exhaust an individual litigant, but also controlled vast amounts of technical expertise on the mechanical aspects the consumer was challenging. Without the possibility of double damages and reasonable attorneys' fees, few consumers would bring such actions.

Chrysler made one last argument, contending that because it offered to provide Hughes with a new vehicle 35 days after the deadline, the pecuniary loss should be limited to the out-of-pocket expenditures Hughes made during those 35 days.

The court found no merit in this argument. The court explained that if it were to accept Chrysler's approach, a manufacturer could routinely refuse to provide a replacement vehicle to a consumer in order to wait and see whether the consumer would actually file suit. The statute clearly required the manufacturer to respond within 30 days, and the court simply refused to rewrite it.

Chrysler then asked the court to consider whether the trial court erroneously exercised its discretion by awarding Hughes the sum of $35,141 in attorney's fees. Chrysler claimed that Hughes's counsel spent an unreasonable amount of time on the case and that the total amount billed exceeded that charged by other attorneys doing similar work.

After looking at the issue, the appellate court concluded that the trial court did not erroneously exercise its discretion by awarding attorney fees. The trial court had conducted an exhaustive review of the fees, and its determination was discretionary.

As a result, the judgment providing double damages for Hughes—and the judgment for attorney's fees in favor of his lawyer—would remain untouched.

13

An Expensive Lesson

Practice Pointer

Let the manufacturer beware: a manufacturer that fails to promptly comply with a consumer's legitimate demand under the lemon law assumes the risk of paying twice the vehicle's full purchase price and other costs listed in the statute, including sales tax, finance charges, attorney fees, and other costs, even if the resulting award seems vastly excessive under the circumstances.

In other words, when parties cannot agree on the correct amount of a refund, the manufacturer can either pay the amount demanded by the purchaser within the 30-day period or pay the amount that the manufacturer deems appropriate within the 30-day period. *Negotiating with the consumer regarding the amount of the refund and the return of the vehicle is not a viable alternative to those narrow options.*

In the case that follows—*James Michael Leasing Co., LLC v. PACCAR INC., d/b/a Kenworth Truck Company*, 772 F,3d 815(7th Cir. 2014)—the court is quick to note that it does not endorse the consumer's confusing conduct, and that both parties engaged in gamesmanship that turned a fairly routine business transaction into unnecessary controversy.

But most lemon laws undoubtedly express a strong preference for the interests of consumers over those of manufacturers. And even though the consumer is a reasonably sophisticated business entity, it is nonetheless entitled to the full protection of the lemon law statute.

The result reached by the trial court in this lemon law case was undoubtedly a harsh one—a truck manufacturer was held liable to a consumer for more than $200,000, even though the parties' initial dispute involved a mileage allowance of less than $4,000.

In confirming the verdict, the appellate court reasoned that previous judicial decisions had clearly laid out the policy of the lemon law statute to impose harsh penalties on manufacturers to ensure that they voluntarily complied with the 30-day time limit.

In this particular case, James Michael Leasing Company, LLC, purchased a brand-new 2008 Kenworth T800 semi-truck from a Milwaukee dealership known as PACCAR, Incorporated for the sum of $135,847.00. The truck had an extended warranty.

Slightly less than four years and 3,000 miles after its purchase, the leasing company concluded that the truck was a lemon, and accordingly, the leasing company sought a refund from PACCAR pursuant to the state's lemon law. PACCAR agreed to refund the purchase price, but the parties' dealings began to turn south when a dispute arose concerning reimbursement of a $53 title fee.

This seemingly insignificant quibble eventually escalated into a lawsuit over the "reasonable allowance for use" to which PACCAR was entitled for the truck's return, and the trial court awarded James Michael Leasing an incredible sum for a truck purchased for slightly less than $136,000—an interest-bearing judgment of $369,196.06, plus $157,697.25 in attorneys' fees!

PACCAR contended that it had complied with all relevant provisions of the lemon law and that the trial court erred in calculating the leasing company's pecuniary loss.

A few facts are in order. After experiencing trouble with the truck over the next four years and 3,076 miles, James Michael Leasing Company sent PACCAR a notice seeking refund of the purchase price and other amounts due under the lemon law.

PACCAR received the notice on June 7, 2011, triggering the 30-day period in which PACCAR was required to "accept return of the motor vehicle and refund to the consumer and to any holder of a perfected security interest in the consumer's motor vehicle, as their interest may appear, the full purchase price plus any sales tax, finance charge, amount paid by the consumer at the point of sale and collateral costs, less a reasonable allowance for use."

For its part, the leasing company, upon receipt of the refund, was obligated to return the truck to PACCAR and take any steps necessary to transfer title back to PACCAR. The 30-day period was scheduled to end on July 7, 2011.

On June 28, 2011, PACCAR sent an e-mail to the leasing company stating that PACCAR would issue a refund for the sum of $117,741.85, calculated as follows:

Purchase price, inclusive of federal excise tax: $135,847.00

(Plus) Collateral costs: $11,764.87

(Plus) Interest: $31,777.03

For a total of: $179,388.90

(Less) Lien payoff through June 30, 2011: $61,647.05

Total amount due to James Michael Leasing: $117,741.85

The next day, PACCAR informed the leasing company that it would mail two checks to the leasing company. One of the checks, in the amount of $61,647.05, was intended to fulfill PACCAR's obligation to pay off the lien.

The other check, in the amount of $117,741.85, represented PACCAR's calculation of the amount the leasing company was due.

The leasing company responded that same day and commented that the refund was deficient by $53, the amount of a title fee the leasing company paid when it purchased the truck. The leasing company further advised PACCAR that it did not want the responsibility of paying off the lien.

On June 30, PACCAR stated that the leasing company would add the disputed $53 to the leasing company's refund. PACCAR advised the leasing company, however, that the $53 increase in the refund would be tempered by a $3,751.24 "reasonable use allowance" deduction that PACCAR calculated by multiplying what it deemed to be the full purchase price of the truck ($121,952.00, the invoice price, minus the federal excise tax of $13,895.00) by 3,076, the number of miles the truck had been driven before a problem was reported, and then dividing the result by 100,000.

After the $53 title fee was added and the $3,751.24 reasonable use allowance was deducted, the new amount PACCAR planned to refund to the leasing company was $114,043.61.

PACCAR advised the leasing company that a check for that amount would be delivered on July 1. The leasing company told PACCAR that the leasing company would return the truck on July 5. The leasing company did not object to the amount of the refund check or to PACCAR's calculation of the reasonable use allowance.

On July 1, the PACCAR representative delivered the check to the leasing company, which rejected the $114,043.61 refund check, asserting that the amount was incorrect but offering no further explanation.

Four days later, on July 5, the first business day following the Independence Day holiday weekend, the leasing company advised PACCAR for the first time that the use allowance was excessive and proposed an alternative deduction of 11.9 cents per mile (or $364.26, rather than the $3,751.24 PACCAR had deducted).

The next day, July 6, the leasing company returned the truck to the dealership. PACCAR informed the leasing company that it understood the return of the truck to constitute an acceptance of PACCAR's refund in the amount of $114,043.61.

The leasing company stated in an email to PACCAR the next day, which was the final day of the 30-day period:

> In good faith, we parked the truck at the dealer on Tuesday, July 5th, because I said we would go to the dealer on Tuesday with the truck. We expected you to pay us what we had coming.
>
> *The amount of $114,043.61 offered by PACCAR is not acceptable or agreeable. The mileage charge is too high.* I made that clear in our last email as well as previous emails, including my email of July 5th.
>
> Please send James Michael Leasing a check immediately in the sum of $117,425.73. This sum allows for *a mileage charge of $369.12* per my last email. You may deliver the check to our business. (Emphasis added)

PACCAR responded to the leasing company by email later that day, expressing confusion as to why the leasing company returned the truck.

PACCAR continued:

> Since James Michael Leasing will not agree to accept the check in the amount of $114,043.61 along with Kenworth direct payoff of the remaining PACCAR Financial lien balance in the amount of $61,868.30 to resolve this complaint, *then James Michael*

> *Leasing needs to pick up the truck* from the Oak Creek, Wisconsin dealership as soon as possible. Any delay in picking up the truck may result in the dealer charging James Michael Leasing storage fees. (Emphasis added)

PACCAR's email was the last conversation in the parties' negotiations. The leasing company eventually retrieved the truck and filed suit.

The trial court concluded that PACCAR violated the lemon law by failing to pay off the leasing company's lien. The court reasoned that "the only thing the consumer must do to trigger the manufacturer's obligation to issue a refund and pay off the lien within 30 days is offer to transfer title of the vehicle to the manufacturer."

Because the leasing company had fulfilled this requirement on June 7, the court concluded that PACCAR had 30 days—until July 7—to perform its statutory duties of issuing a refund check and paying off the lien, which it failed to do.

As a result, the court found that the leasing company was entitled to damages provided by the lemon law: "twice the amount of any pecuniary loss, together with costs, disbursements and reasonable attorney fees." The court deemed the leasing company's "pecuniary loss" to include the full purchase price of the truck.

The parties eventually stipulated that the leasing company's "pecuniary loss" was $184,598.03. This figure included the $135,847.00 full purchase price, $53.00 in title fees, $11,767.87 in collateral costs, and $38,805.16 that the leasing company paid on its lien, less a reasonable use allowance of $1,875.00.

The trail district court then doubled this "pecuniary loss" to arrive at a damages award of $369,196.06. The court added $2,730.24 in prejudgment interest through October 31, 2011, the date the leasing company made a settlement offer; $4,627.90 in statutory costs; and $2,029.45 in litigation costs.

The court also awarded the leasing company 5 percent interest on the damages from November 1, 2011, forward, and $146,081.25 in attorneys' fees through May 15, 2013. The court later awarded the leasing company an additional $11,616 in attorneys' fees, for a total fee award of $157,697.25.

The trial court thus entered judgment in favor of the leasing company in the amount of $536,280.90 and 5 percent interest on the amount of $369,196.06 from November 1, 2011, until that amount was paid.

PACCAR appealed, contending that its offers to the leasing company and assurances that it would pay off the lien were sufficient to satisfy its obligations under the lemon law.

PACCAR further contended that:

- It was not required to pay off the lien until the leasing company accepted its proffered refund check,
- Its calculation of the reasonable use allowance was in compliance with the strictures of the lemon law, and
- The leasing company's "pecuniary loss" was limited to the difference between the amount PACCAR tendered within the statutory period and what was properly due and owing under the statute.

The parties agreed that the leasing company was a "consumer" within the meaning of the lemon law and that the truck at issue was in fact a lemon. Under the plain language of the lemon law, the leasing company had a right to seek from PACCAR either replacement of the truck or a refund. The leasing company chose the refund and made an offer to transfer title of the truck to PACCAR.

The leasing company's offer triggered an obligation for PACCAR to do the following within 30 days:

> Accept return of the motor vehicle and *refund to the consumer* and to any holder of a perfected security interest in the consumer's motor vehicle, as their interest may appear, *the full purchase price* plus any sales tax, finance charge, amount paid by the consumer at the point of sale and collateral costs, *less a reasonable allowance for use*. Under this provision, *a reasonable allowance for use* may not exceed the amount obtained by multiplying the full purchase price of the motor vehicle by a fraction, the denominator of which is 100,000 or, for a motorcycle, 20,000, and the numerator of which is the number of miles the motor vehicle was driven before the consumer first reported the nonconformity to the motor vehicle dealer. (Emphasis added)

When the manufacturer provided the refund, the consumer was then obligated to return the vehicle to the manufacturer with the certificate of title and other endorsements.

The lemon law also authorized consumers to recover for any damages caused by a violation, and instructed the court to award to a prevailing consumer "twice the amount of any pecuniary loss, together with costs, disbursements and reasonable attorney fees, and any equitable relief the court determines appropriate."

In describing the particular statute at issue, the court observed that this lemon law was particularly pro-consumer in a number of ways. The law permitted the recovery of double damages, attorneys' fees, and costs, and it lacked both affirmative defenses and mechanisms to obtain sanctions against consumers who brought claims in bad faith. In other words, the statute squarely placed the burden on the manufacturer to provide a refund within the 30-day statutory period.

PACCAR contended that it met its burden under the statute by timely tendering the $114,043.61 check to the leasing company and by accepting responsibility for paying off (but not actually paying off) the leasing company's lien.

The court pointed out that the plain text of the lemon law obligated manufacturers like PACCAR to "refund to the consumer and to any holder of a perfected security interest in the consumer's motor vehicle, as their interest may appear, the full purchase price plus any sales tax, finance charge, amount paid by the consumer at the point of sale and collateral costs, less a reasonable allowance for use."

This language of the lemon law required manufacturers to actually refund the money due within 30 days—not simply to *agree* to do so—and the statute required manufacturers to refund the money directly to the security interest holder rather than leaving the consumer to sort it out with the lender.

The court was unpersuaded by PACCAR's argument that the leasing company's rejection of the refund amounts—coupled with the leasing company's unequivocal pronouncement that it would not return the vehicle—relieved PACCAR of its duty to pay off the lien. The lemon law obligated the consumer to return the vehicle or certificate of title to the manufacturer only when the manufacturer provided the new motor vehicle or refund.

Thus, the leasing company's refusal to return the vehicle did not absolve PACCAR of its duty to fulfill its statutory obligations. The parties' duties were undoubtedly linked, but the link was a sequential one pursuant to which the manufacturer had to take the lead.

PACCAR did not argue that the leasing company acted to intentionally thwart its attempts to comply with the lemon law. In the absence of such a contention, the manufacturer had no excuses for noncompliance.

In other words, when the parties could not agree on the correct amount of a refund, the manufacturer had two options:

- Pay the amount demanded by the purchaser within the 30-day period, or
- Pay the amount that the manufacturer deemed appropriate within the 30-day period.

Negotiating with the consumer regarding the amount of the refund and the return of the vehicle was not a viable alternative to those narrow options.

In reaching this conclusion, the court was quick to note that it did not endorse the leasing company's confusing conduct, which neglected to clarify its rationale for declining PACCAR's proffered checks and which inexplicably returned the truck.

In fact, both parties engaged in a gamesmanship that turned a fairly routine business transaction into unnecessary controversy. The lemon law expressed a strong preference for the interests of consumers over the interests of manufacturers. And while the leasing company was a reasonably sophisticated business entity, it was nonetheless entitled to the full protection of the lemon law statute.

PACCAR contended that the leasing company's "pecuniary loss" was limited to the difference between the parties' calculated use allowances. The statute was silent as to whether pecuniary loss included the purchase price of the vehicle. But the state supreme court had held that "the legislature intended to include the purchase price of the car as pecuniary damages."

The court explained that if the contrary conclusion were reached, the lemon law would:

- Fail in its purpose to significantly improve upon the remedies available to consumers,
- Manufacturers would have little, if any, incentive to promptly comply with the statute, and
- Consumers would have far less motivation to seek compensation for violations of their statutory rights.

PACCAR's argument that the consumer's pecuniary loss should be limited to the out-of-pocket expenditures the consumer made was rejected by the court.

The court recognized that the atypical nature of the vehicle controversy at issue in the present case led to an award that far exceeded the amounts awarded in the usual run-of-the-mill lemon law controversy.

Statutes of general applicability, the court lamented, are often "blunt instruments," and a manufacturer who failed to timely comply with a consumer's demand runs big risks—like having to pay twice the vehicle's full purchase price plus attorneys' fees and other costs.

14

Subjective Standard

Practice Pointer

The courts are clear that the lemon law's purpose of protecting consumers while preventing frivolous litigation is best served by an *objective test, which ensures that consumers are adequately protected and at the same time prevents lawsuits over cosmetic or trivial defects.*

In the case that follows—*Iams v. Daimler Chrysler Corporation*, 883 N.E.2d 466 (Ohio 2007)—the consumer argues that the statutory phrase "to the consumer" indicates that the "substantial impairment" of the nonconformity is a subjective one and that the motor vehicle's diminished use, value, or safety should be measured from the perspective of the consumer. The manufacturer urges that it is also reasonable to conclude that the phrase "to the consumer" simply means that the consumer is the party affected by the alleged defect.

Most courts conclude that the term is inherently ambiguous and that the objective test best serves the lemon law's purpose of protecting consumers while preventing frivolous litigation. The lemon law was not enacted to remedy "cosmetic or other trivial" reasons, and an objective test best prevents lawsuits over cosmetic or trivial defects.

If a subjective standard were applied, practically every vehicle with a defect would be considered a lemon, and it would expand the lemon law's application beyond its legislative intent.

Craig Iams purchased a new 2005 Jeep Wrangler with a three-year or 36,000-mile warranty. A few months later, he noticed that the rear lift-gate latch would suddenly pop open when the doors were closed. The result was a lot of road noise.

Shortly thereafter, Iams brought the Wrangler to a Chrysler dealership in Ohio for repair. The issue was resolved for a brief period of time, but Iams had to bring the car back to the dealer for the same problem three more times.

Frustrated, Iams then filed suit against Chrysler pursuant to the state's lemon law. Eventually the trial court granted Chrysler's motion for summary judgment and dismissed Iams's claims.

To prevail under the lemon law, the consumer had to establish that:

- The consumer was the owner of a vehicle covered by the warranty,
- The vehicle did not conform to the standards of the warranty,
- The consumer reported the nonconformity to the manufacturer within a year of the date of delivery or the first 18,000 miles of operation, whichever occurred earlier, and
- After a reasonable number of repair attempts, the manufacturer was unable to repair the defect that substantially impaired the use, safety, or value of the motor vehicle.

Iams argued that he presented evidence sufficient to establish a valid lemon law claim. Chrysler maintained that Iams failed to show that the vehicle defect was "nonconforming" as defined under the lemon law. Specifically, Chrysler argued that the defect did not substantially impair the "use, safety, or value" of the vehicle and that the substantial impairment requirement was an objective one.

Iams countered that the substantial impairment requirement was in fact a subjective one to be measured from the individual consumer's perspective. In support of his proposition, Iams pointed to the statutory language, which defined nonconformity as "any defect or condition that substantially impairs the use, value, or safety of a motor vehicle *to the consumer* and does not conform to the express warranty of the manufacturer or distributor" (emphasis added).

The language of the lemon law provided (*emphasis added*):

(A) If a new motor vehicle does not *conform to any applicable express warranty* and the consumer reports the *nonconformity* to the manufacturer, its agent, or its authorized dealer during the period of one year following the date of original delivery or during the first 18,000 miles of operation, whichever is earlier, the manufacturer, its agent, or its authorized dealer shall make any repairs as are necessary *to conform the vehicle to such express warranty*, notwithstanding the fact that the repairs are made after the expiration of the appropriate time period.

(B) If the manufacturer, its agent, or its authorized dealer is unable to conform the motor vehicle *to any applicable express warranty* by repairing or correcting any defect or condition that substantially impairs the use, safety, or value of the motor vehicle *to the consumer* after a reasonable number of repair attempts, the manufacturer shall, *at the consumers option*, and *replace the motor vehicle with a new motor vehicle* acceptable to the consumer or *accept return of the vehicle from the consumer and refund* each of the following:

(1) The *full purchase price* including, but not limited to, charges for undercoating, transportation, and installed options;

(2) All *collateral charges*, including but not limited to, sales tax, license and registration fees, and similar government charges;

(3) All *finance charges* incurred by the consumer;

(4) All *incidental damages*, including any reasonable fees charged by the lender for making or canceling the loan. (Emphasis added)

The dispute in this case was whether the Wrangler's defect rendered the vehicle nonconforming as defined in the statute. Iams argued that the plain meaning of the phrase "to the consumer" in the statute indicated that the substantial impairment requirement was a subjective one and that the motor vehicle's diminished use, value, or safety should be measured from the perspective of the consumer.

The court disagreed that Iams's interpretation was necessarily the meaning of the statutory language. The court noted that it was also reasonable to conclude that the phrase "to the consumer" simply meant that the consumer must be the party affected by the alleged defect.

In the end, the court concluded that the term was inherently ambiguous. When the word "to" precedes a personal object word, it can be translated as "in the opinion of" a particular person, resulting in a subjective standard, as Iams argued.

Or, the court said, the phrase could mean that the person was affected by the subject matter of the sentence, resulting in an objective standard, not a subjective one, as Chrysler argued.

Given that there were at least two reasonable interpretations of the phrase "to the consumer," the court moved to an analysis of the case law, which, confusingly enough, featured cases requiring both subjective and objective views.

The court eventually concluded that an objective test best served the lemon law's purpose of protecting consumers while preventing frivolous litigation. The lemon law was undoubtedly a consumer protection statute, but the statute was not enacted to remedy "cosmetic or other trivial" reasons. An objective test best ensured that consumers were adequately protected, and at the same time it prevented lawsuits over cosmetic or trivial defects.

If a subjective standard were applied, practically every vehicle with a defect would be considered a lemon, and manufacturers would rarely win once the consumer demonstrated that the vehicle was under warranty and the defect was timely and properly presented for repairs the required number of times. The subjective standard would exponentially expand the lemon law's application beyond its legislative intent.

Furthermore, application of the lemon law to subjectively trivial or cosmetic reasons would be inequitable. Purchasers would be awarded a windfall for minor defects in their vehicles. In the words of the court, the legislature surely did not intend such a harsh remedy for objectively minor defects.

In the present case, the lift-gate latch opened due to the air pressure differential when a door of the vehicle was closed. The parties agreed that the problem could be remedied by simply cracking the window of either door before closing it. When the lift-gate latch was open, the vehicle was noisier, but the defect, though bothersome, did not substantially impair the vehicle's use, value, or safety for a reasonable person.

First, the problem did not affect the Wrangler as a whole. The lift-gate latch was part of a removable hard top and did not interfere with the mechanical functioning of the vehicle.

Second, the problem did not affect the Wrangler's essential design and purpose. It only increased wind noise. Most Wranglers were not purchased for their quiet, comfortable ride, but rather for their rough-and-ready design. Consumers typically understood that the Wrangler design resulted in a louder, rougher ride compared with other vehicles.

Third, the defective lift-gate latch was minor and did not constitute a safety concern. According to Iams's expert, the rear window glass lifted, at most, 2 or 3 inches and then settled back in position with only a 1/8 inch gap between the window and the frame. The spare tire and brake-light assembly on the rear tailgate prevented the window from completely opening, and even Iams's expert admitted that the lift-gate latch was not a safety issue.

When asked if there was any other problem associated with the defective latch, Iams admitted that he never had any problems with water leaking underneath the hatch.

The court therefore concluded that Iams's lemon law claim lacked merit. The case presented a single defect, which was not serious in nature. The popping lift-gate latch was annoying, but the problem could be easily remedied by simply cracking the window to one of the Wrangler's doors before closing it. The court was not persuaded that the defect was serious or a substantial impairment to the vehicle's use, value, or safety.

Therefore, the next time he drove the Wrangler, Mr. Iams would have to crack the window a bit and put up with a little road noise.

15

Preexisting Conditions

PRACTICE POINTER

Nothing in the plain language of the lemon law requires *that the consumer be unaware of the warranty nonconformity* before accepting delivery of the vehicle in order for the law to apply. In other words, the statute *does not limit its applicability to hidden vehicle nonconformities*. Had the legislature intended to so restrict its application, it could easily have done so, but it did not.

The protections of the lemon law cannot be waived, and the contention that the law does not apply when the consumer is aware of the defect is in effect a rule of waiver by notice.

In the case that follows—*Dieter v. Chrysler Corporation*, 610 N.W.2d 832 (Wis. 2000)—the court explains that the purpose of the lemon law is to reduce the inconvenience, expense, and frustration for consumers who purchase defective vehicles and to provide an incentive to a manufacturer to restore consumers to their positions at the time of the purchase. The fact that the consumer is aware of a defect does not prevent enforcement of the lemon law, particularly when the manufacturer or dealer has promised to remedy the defect.

Kerry Dieter and Donna Hermes bought a brand-new 1996 Dodge Ram pick-up truck from a Chrysler dealership in Troy, Wisconsin, along with several after-market accessories—a tonneau cover, bug deflector, fender shield, and rustproofing—which the dealership installed.

During the installation of the accessories, the dealer unfortunately scratched the truck's paint finish in several places. Before taking delivery of the truck, Dieter and Hermes saw the blemishes and threatened to cancel the sale. The dealer warned them that if they did, it would forfeit their deposit.

The dealer assured Dieter and Hermes, though, that any damage to the truck's finish would be repaired to their satisfaction. After much consternation, Dieter and Hermes finally drove the truck off the lot.

The dealer then arranged for a body repair company to repaint the truck at Chrysler's expense. Dieter and Hermes instructed the repair company not to "buff" the finish after repainting, but the company did so anyway, leaving unsatisfactory swirls in the truck's finish. The dealership made at least three more attempts have the truck fixed (all at Chrysler's expense).

Dissatisfied with the end result, Dieter and Hermes sought relief under the lemon law. On November 19, 1996, their attorney sent a demand letter to Chrysler stating that the truck was a lemon and that they wanted Chrysler to repurchase the vehicle as provided in the lemon law. Chrysler refused to do so, and Dieter and Hermes sued.

The warranty on the truck provided coverage for "any item on the vehicle that is defective in material, workmanship, or factory preparation." The warranty contained exclusions for damage to the truck due to accidents, abuse, negligence, misuse, repairs necessitated by improper maintenance, modification of the truck, or the installation of non-Chrysler parts. There was an exception to the exclusion, however, for "genuine MOPAR [a portmanteau of the words "motor" and "parts"] accessories approved by Chrysler for dealer installation."

Chrysler moved for summary judgment, initially claiming that the accessories installed by the dealership were *not* Chrysler MOPAR parts and therefore *not* covered by the warranty or the lemon law.

The trial court granted summary judgment for Chrysler, but Dieter and Hermes objected that Chrysler had *not* proven that the accessories were *not* Chrysler MOPAR parts. The trial court concluded that regardless of whether the parts in question were Chrysler MOPAR parts, the lemon law was inapplicable because the parts were not the problem, but rather their installation, which was the responsibility of the dealer rather than the manufacturer. The trial court again granted summary judgment for Chrysler.

On appeal, Chrysler conceded that the accessories were in fact MOPAR parts but continued to argue that it was not responsible for damage caused by the dealer's negligent installation. Chrysler contended (1) that the purpose of the lemon law was to protect consumers from *hidden* defects in their new vehicles and (2) that the statute was therefore not applicable where the consumer was *aware* of nonconformities before delivery but accepted the vehicle nonetheless.

The court first reviewed Chrysler's truck warranty, which provided in part:

> **WHAT'S COVERED:** The "Basic Warranty" covers the cost of all parts and labor needed to repair any item on your truck that's defective in material, workmanship, or factory preparation. *You pay nothing for these repairs.* The "Basic Warranty" covers every Chrysler supplied part of your truck EXCEPT its tires and cellular telephone. (Emphasis added)

There was an exclusion for non-Chrysler parts and repairs occasioned by the installation of non-Chrysler parts:

> **WHAT'S NOT COVERED:** *Your Chrysler Warranties don't cover any part which is not a Chrysler supplied part.* These warranties also don't cover the costs of any repairs or adjustments that might be caused by or needed because of the use or installation of non-Chrysler parts, equipment, materials or additives. (Emphasis added)

But there was an exception to the exclusion:

> Examples of the types of alterations that are not covered include, but are not limited to, the installation of accessories (*except for genuine MOPAR accessories approved by Chrysler for dealer installation*) such as sun roofs, window tinting, trailer hitches, theft alarm systems, rustproofing or other protection products, or the use of any refrigerant other than that approved by Chrysler. (Emphasis added)

Therefore, repairs regarding the installation of "genuine MOPAR accessories approved by Chrysler for dealer installation" *were* covered by the warranty because they were clearly excepted from the exclusion of the warranty. The defect in this particular vehicle—scratches to its paint finish—resulted from the installation of genuine MOPAR parts by a Chrysler dealer. As a result, the court concluded, there *was* in fact warranty coverage.

Chrysler then argued, however, that the warranty did not apply because the damage to the truck occurred *before* the beginning date of the warranty (in this case, the date of delivery).

The court saw a problem with this argument: the warranty contained no time limitation relating to the date that the defect or damage occurred. The warranty simply covered repair costs that were incurred during the warranty period for qualifying defects and damage.

Chrysler next argued that because Dieter and Hermes could have rejected delivery of the truck once they discovered the scratches, but instead chose to negotiate with the dealer regarding repair, their remedy was with the dealer—not the manufacturer.

In the present case, the damage in question met the definition of "what's covered," read together with the exception to "what's not covered," in the warranty, and the repair costs were incurred during the warranty period. When this was the case, the court held that the customer should pay "nothing for these repairs," according to the plain language of the warranty.

The court of appeals, however, held that the lemon law did *not* apply when the consumer was previously *aware* of the defect in the vehicle. The court based this conclusion in the remedial purposes of the lemon law:

> Our conclusion that the Lemon Law covers only those *defects that manifest themselves to the consumer after delivery* is in keeping with the purpose behind the Lemon Law. The Lemon Law was enacted to protect the consumer who makes a large investment in a brand new vehicle only to find that the vehicle is a dud. *He or she drives the new vehicle home, expecting problem-free dependability*. Problems develop, but it is too late for the consumer to back out of the deal. The Lemon Law protects this consumer from a seller who is unable or unwilling to repair the defective vehicle. (Emphasis added)

Here the alleged defects in the truck were apparent when the consumer accepted the vehicle. The consumer had the chance to back out before the sale was final and pursue a refund of their deposit, but instead, the consumer negotiated further with the dealership and ultimately accepted the vehicle subject to the dealership's promise to repair.

In other words, the consumer's dissatisfaction had nothing to do with Chrysler, and the fact that the dealership was a Chrysler dealer did not bring these visible, predelivery defects within the purview of the lemon law.

The appellate court remarked that the lemon law did not, on its face, speak to whether the vehicle defect must be "hidden" or whether the consumer was unaware of its existence at the time of delivery in order to trigger relief. The relevant lemon law language stated:

> If a new motor vehicle *does not conform to an applicable express warranty and the consumer reports the nonconformity to the manufacturer*, the motor vehicle lessor or any of the manufacturer's authorized motor vehicle dealers and makes the motor vehicle available for repair before the expiration of the warranty or one year after first delivery of the motor vehicle to a consumer, whichever is sooner, the nonconformity shall be repaired. (Emphasis added)

The statute defined a "nonconformity" as:

> A condition or defect which *substantially impairs the use, value or safety of a motor vehicle*, and is *covered by an express warranty* applicable to the motor vehicle or to a component of the motor vehicle, but does not include a condition or defect which is the result of abuse, neglect or unauthorized modification or alteration of the motor vehicle by a consumer. (Emphasis added)

The appellate court's decision in favor of the manufacturer was then appealed to the state supreme court, which held to the contrary—that nothing in the plain language of the lemon law *required* that the consumer be unaware of the nonconformity before accepting delivery of the vehicle in order for the law to apply.

In other words, nothing in the statute limited its applicability to *hidden* vehicle nonconformities. Had the legislature intended to so restrict the law's application, the legislature could easily have done so, but it did not.

Furthermore, the legislature explicitly provided that the protections of the lemon law could *not* be waived. In the eyes of the supreme court, the court of appeals' conclusion that the law did not apply when the consumer was aware of the defect was in effect a rule of waiver by notice.

The supreme court reminded the parties that the lemon law was enacted to provide consumers with remedies beyond the "inadequate, uncertain and expensive remedies of the Uniform Commercial Code or the Magnuson–Moss Warranty Act." The lemon law was a warranty enforcement statute—"a self-enforcing consumer law that provided 'important rights to motor vehicle owners.'"

The purpose of the lemon law, the supreme court reiterated, was to reduce the inconvenience, expense, and frustration of consumers who purchased defective vehicles and to provide an incentive to the manufacturer to restore consumers of such a vehicle to their position at the time of the purchase.

The court concluded that the plain language of Chrysler's warranty provided coverage for damage inflicted by its dealers during the installation of Chrysler-approved MOPAR parts. Chrysler assumed warranty responsibility for repairs necessitated by the installation of MOPAR parts by its dealers, and along with this warranty responsibility came potential lemon law liability.

The court also found, based on its unambiguous language, that the lemon law simply contained no "hidden defect" or "lack of knowledge" requirement.

In other words, a few scratches on a vehicle—even those that were obvious on the showroom floor—could not emasculate the strong arm of the lemon law.

16

Defining "Comparable"

Practice Pointer

Lemon laws typically provide that if the warranty nonconformity is not repaired, the manufacturer must accept the return of the vehicle and, if the consumer chooses, replace the nonconforming vehicle with a comparable vehicle. This applies to all accessories as well.

Most courts have held that *transferring nondefective automobile accessories into replacement vehicles is not contemplated within the statute* or consistent with its public policy of returning consumers back to where they thought they were when they first purchased that new vehicle.

In the case that follows—*Kiss v. General Motor Corporation*, 630 N.W.2d 742 (Wis. 2001)—it was emphasized that when the consumer purchased the vehicle, he thought he was getting a brand new vehicle with full warranties. If an accessory was transferred to the new vehicle, the consumer would receive an old accessory with an expiring warranty and potential problems.

Peter Kiss purchased a new 1997 GMC Sierra 3500 HD Tow Truck from an authorized General Motors dealership in West Bend, Wisconsin. The truck also contained a separate Vulcan 882 towing package, manufactured by Miller Industries, which the dealer installed.

Shortly after Kiss took delivery of the vehicle, he experienced substantial problems with the performance of the GMC truck but not with the Vulcan towing package.

In October 1997, Kiss filed a *pro se* lemon law claim against General Motors. On December 15, the informal dispute settlement tribunal issued a decision in favor of Kiss, requiring GM to replace the vehicle within 30 days of Kiss's acceptance of its decision.

On January 26, 1998, Kiss accepted the dispute settlement decision, and GM received notification obligating GM to provide a comparable new motor vehicle by mid-March.

During February and March, it became clear that the dealership did not have a new Sierra truck that suited Kiss's preferences. GM offered to manufacture a new truck to meet those specifications (which would take six to eight weeks) and to transfer the old tow unit to the new truck.

Kiss rejected GM's offer. He argued that the settlement decision required GM to replace not only the cab and chassis, but also the towing package. GM contended that the decision required GM to replace *only* the cab and chassis.

Negotiations continued through the summer, and at one point, GM offered to repurchase the tow truck for the full sale price, including the Vulcan towing package. Kiss refused the offer.

On October 13, 1998—a year after his initial claim—Kiss sent a demand letter to GM offering to transfer title in return for a comparable new motor vehicle. The parties were unable to reach an agreement, and Kiss brought suit against GM, alleging that GM failed to timely offer a comparable new motor vehicle and seeking double damages under the lemon law.

On May 6, 1999, GM filed a motion for summary judgment, claiming that it had fully complied with the lemon law by making a *replacement* vehicle available to Kiss. On December 15, the trial court ruled in GM's favor and dismissed Kiss's claims. Kiss appealed.

The language "comparable new motor vehicle" in the state's lemon law statute provided in part:

> If after a reasonable attempt to repair the nonconformity is not repaired, the manufacturer shall . . .
>
> At the direction of a consumer . . .
>
> Accept return of the motor vehicle and *replace the motor vehicle with a comparable new motor vehicle* and refund any collateral costs. (Emphasis added)

Kiss contended that GM never fully complied with its obligation under the lemon law because it offered only a new cab and chassis along with the transfer of the old tow package from the lemon.

According to Kiss, this was not a "comparable new motor vehicle" because the statute did not contemplate transferring used parts and accessories from the lemon to the replacement vehicle. Kiss's underlying claim was based on the vehicle itself, which was entirely under GM's warranty.

GM countered that the lemon law did not require a manufacturer to replace a tow unit that the manufacturer did not manufacture, sell, or warrant.

The court observed that the plain language of the statute did not define the word "comparable." The court had previously interpreted "comparable" to mean "a similar model vehicle with similar features, such as the type of engine, transmission, brakes, seat upholstery and accessories."

The statute provided that if the nonconformity was not repaired, the manufacturer had to accept the return of the vehicle and, at the consumer's request, either (1) replace the vehicle or (2) refund the consumer's money paid at the point of sale.

Had Kiss elected *refund* of the purchase price at point of sale, he would have received an amount in excess of $43,000.00. This figure reflected the value of the cab and chassis and the Vulcan towing equipment. And during negotiations, GM had offered to repurchase the vehicle from Kiss for $44,751.72.

Had Kiss chosen the *replacement* provision of the lemon law, he would have been entitled only to the cab and chassis, a value of about $24,000.

In spite of this substantial difference, Kiss steadfastly requested *replacement* instead of a refund. The anomalous result in values, the court pointed out, would render the replacement option a nullity for consumers who purchased dealer-added accessories not manufactured or warranted by the manufacturer.

Furthermore, the court said, transferring the current tow package would not place Kiss in the same position he thought he was in at the point of sale. When Kiss purchased the truck, he thought he was getting a brand new tow truck with full warranties. If the tow unit was transferred to a new cab and chassis, he would receive an old tow package with an expiring warranty. The transfer of the old tow package also opened the door to a number of troublesome possibilities related to compromising the integrity of the tow unit or replacement vehicle.

Simply put, the court held that transferring nondefective automobile accessories into replacement vehicles was not contemplated by the lemon law statute and was inconsistent with its public policy of returning "unfortunate consumers back to where they thought they were when they first purchased that new automobile."

The court also reasoned that the plain language of the dispute settlement decision unambiguously required GM to provide Kiss with a new tow unit as well as the new cab and chassis. The dispute settlement decision expressly stated:

> GM shall replace the 1997 GMC Sierra ("vehicle") owned/leased by Kiss within 30 days after the manufacturer is notified that the customer has accepted this decision, *with a new motor vehicle that is substantially identical to the replaced vehicle* (not including any modifications or additions after the vehicle's purchase or lease), and of the same model year as the replaced vehicle. (Emphasis added)

By the terms of the dispute settlement agreement, GM was excused from replacing only those modifications or additions installed after Kiss purchased the vehicle. Further clarification was found in the "Reasons for Decision" in the informal settlement decision (*emphasis added*):

> Was the alleged problem caused by abuse, neglect, or unauthorized modification or alteration of the vehicle by a consumer?
>
> No. This vehicle was sold as a tow truck: The tow package (GM authorized) *was added by an authorized dealer prior to customer's purchase/acceptance of unit.*

The court held that a substantially identical replacement vehicle was one that possessed *all* the modifications/additions that the vehicle possessed as of the date of purchase.

In this case, the informal dispute settlement tribunal explicitly recognized that the tow unit was installed by the dealer prior to purchase. Therefore, GM had to replace the tow truck in order to provide Kiss with a new motor vehicle that was substantially identical to the replaced vehicle.

Because GM never offered to provide a new tow unit along with a new cab and chassis, either after the dispute settlement decision or after the October 1998 demand letter, the court concluded that GM had failed to comply with the lemon law.

The question was then whether Kiss could pursue a lemon law claim to enforce the dispute settlement award against GM.

GM argued that Kiss's acceptance of the informal dispute settlement award barred suit under the lemon law. GM conceded that if Kiss had rejected the award, his recourse would have been to pursue a lemon law claim for double damages and attorney's fees.

However, there was no precedent governing appeal from a settlement decision after its acceptance. GM contended that the state arbitration act was the only available remedy for enforcement of a lemon law dispute settlement award.

Kiss countered that his acceptance of the dispute settlement decision did not preclude suit under the lemon law because that law specifically prohibited any waiver or limitation of a consumer's rights. Forcing Kiss to resort to arbitration, which did not allow an award for double damages or attorney's fees, would improperly limit Kiss's remedies. Kiss contended that this was a result that would defeat the purpose of the lemon law.

The court noted that the statutes in question were neither vague nor ambiguous, nor did they overlap. The state arbitration act related to the relief to which a party to arbitration was entitled. Under its provisions, a party was limited to enforcement, vacation, or modification of an arbitration award. The arbitration act did not provide any additional relief to a party who was aggrieved by the failure of another party to comply with an arbitration decision.

The arbitration act, unlike the lemon law, did not permit a party to recover attorney's fees and costs. The arbitration act therefore would provide only limited relief to a consumer who was required to resort to an informal dispute settlement procedure prior to filing suit under the lemon law.

The lemon law, on the other hand, was a remedial statute that sought to provide an incentive for a manufacturer to return the purchaser of a new vehicle to the position the purchaser was in at the time the vehicle was purchased. The incentive included an award of double damages and attorney' fees when the manufacturer failed to comply with the statute in a timely manner.

If the manufacturer provided an informal dispute settlement mechanism, the consumer had to use it before filing a lemon law claim. In this case, Kiss resorted to the informal dispute procedure as he was required to do.

The court found no persuasive authority to support GM's position that enforcement of the informal settlement decision was limited to the arbitration statute. The lemon law did not, on its face, speak to whether a consumer was barred from pursuing a lemon law claim after resorting to the dispute settlement procedure. Nor was the arbitration act referred to anywhere in the lemon law statute.

In fact, the word "arbitration" did not appear in the lemon law statute either. Nothing implied that consumers who accepted a settlement decision terminated their lemon law rights. Had the legislature intended to restrict application of the lemon law remedies in this way, it could easily have done so.

Furthermore, the legislature explicitly provided that the protections afforded by the lemon law could not be waived. GM's position that Kiss's acceptance of the dispute settlement decision limited his recourse to arbitration essentially involved a waiver of lemon law remedies. The court agreed with Kiss that this would contravene the nonwaiver provision of the lemon law.

The court held that the lemon law was a "stand-alone" statute that was not dependent upon or qualified by other statutes, and that therefore consumers' obligations under the lemon law could not be expanded.

In the end, the lemon law prevailed. GM had violated the lemon law by failing to provide a comparable new motor vehicle to Kiss in accordance with the settlement decision, and Kiss was entitled to seek enforcement of that decision under the statute.

17

Available for Repair

PRACTICE POINTER

Under most lemon laws, a consumer must promptly report the vehicle nonconformity to the manufacturer or to one of its authorized dealers in order to make sure that the manufacturer learns of the problem.

To take advantage of the law, the consumer must then make the vehicle "available for repair," which obligates the manufacturer to repair the nonconformity. The flexible language *preserves lemon law protection when the manufacturer directs the consumer to a repair shop other than the manufacturer's own authorized dealers.*

In the case that follows—*Burzlaff v. Thoroughbred Motorsports, Inc.*, 758 F.3d 841 (7th Cir. 2014)—the manufacturer proposed a narrow interpretation that would allow the consumer to lose the statute's protections by taking the vehicle to a different repair facility, even though directed to do so by the manufacturer.

Not only would such a result raise serious, obvious issues of estoppel, but it would be unjust to the point of absurdity and an invitation to bad-faith conduct by manufacturers.

On October 19, 2009, Ronald Burzlaff purchased a "Stallion" Motor Trike at a total cost of over $35,000 from Thoroughbred Motorsports, a small company based in Texas with only about 20 authorized dealers nationwide.

The Stallion was an unusual vehicle, complete with a steering wheel, heat and air conditioning, and other features not normally found on motorcycles. Burzlaff immediately began to experience problems with the motor trike:

- The motorcycle was delivered without a gas cap and would not start,
- The heating and air conditioning failed,
- The transmission leaked,
- The cooling system leaked,
- Other plugs and seals leaked,
- The steering wheel was loose and the front wheel moved out of alignment, making the vehicle unstable,
- One tire would not hold air,
- The radio did not work, and
- The headlight and taillight sockets were loose.

During its first year, the unreliable Stallion Motor Trike was in various repair shops for a total of 71 days.

In November 2009, Burzlaff contacted Thoroughbred about these various mechanical issues, and Thoroughbred informed Burzlaff he could take the motor trike to a nearby Ford dealer for warranty repairs. Thoroughbred did not specify a particular Ford dealer, so Burzlaff chose Amato Ford, which was located nearby. Although Amato Ford was not a so-called authorized Thoroughbred dealer, Burzlaff knew that it had serviced other Stallions.

Over that first year, Thoroughbred provided Amato Ford with parts to repair Burzlaff's vehicle, and Amato Ford billed the repairs directly to Thoroughbred for payment. Thoroughbred never instructed Amato Ford to stop repairing Burzlaff's vehicle.

Before the end of the first year, Burzlaff met the president and founder of Thoroughbred, Jeffrey Vey, at a motorcycle rally in Wisconsin. Burzlaff complained about the ongoing repairs and asked Vey for a replacement vehicle or a refund of his purchase price. Vey refused, but he did offer to transport the motor trike to the factory in Texas for repairs. Burzlaff followed up with a letter to Vey later that month, but the vehicle was not returned to the factory until some weeks later, more than a year after its purchase.

Six more months passed before the vehicle was returned to Burzlaff, who then filed suit against Thoroughbred alleging violations of the lemon law. The parties stipulated that the pecuniary damages were $35,633.23, the total purchase price of the motor trike.

Burzlaff finally demanded that Thoroughbred replace the vehicle or refund his purchase price. Thoroughbred refused, and another effort to repair the vehicle at the Thoroughbred factory in Texas failed to correct the defects.

Burzlaff then sued Thoroughbred under the state lemon law. The jury found for Burzlaff and awarded double damages plus costs and attorney fees for a total judgment of $94,907.96 under the provisions of the statute.

The statute required the consumer to provide notice of the nonconformity and an opportunity to repair:

> If a new motor vehicle does not conform to an applicable express warranty and the consumer *reports the nonconformity* to the manufacturer, the motor vehicle lessor or any of the manufacturer's authorized motor vehicle dealers and *makes the motor vehicle available for repair* before the expiration of the warranty or one year after first delivery of the motor vehicle to a consumer, whichever is sooner, the *nonconformity shall be repaired.* (Emphasis added)

A nonconformity was defined as "a condition or defect which substantially impairs the use, value or safety of a motor vehicle" and which was covered by an express warranty, but the definition excluded the results of abuse, neglect, or unauthorized modification of the vehicle by the consumer.

If the nonconformity persisted after a "reasonable attempt to repair," the manufacturer had to provide either a full refund or a replacement vehicle. The "reasonable attempt to repair" failed if four attempts to repair the same nonconformity was unsuccessful or if the vehicle was out of service for repairs for 30 days or more in the first year.

The parties agreed that notice of a nonconformity had to be given to "the manufacturer, the motor vehicle lessor, or any of the manufacturer's authorized motor vehicle dealers." Burzlaff did so.

The statute also required the consumer to make the vehicle "available for repair." Thoroughbred contended that if the vehicle was not taken to one of the listed entities for the actual repairs, the lemon law did not apply.

Burzlaff countered that the statute limited only those entities to which notice must be given. He argued that the vehicle had been made "available for repair" once it was taken to any authorized shop, whether or not the shop was also an authorized dealer. The court held that Burzlaff's approach was closer to both the text and purpose of the lemon law.

The text of the lemon law contained fairly strict requirements for who had to receive notice from the consumer, but the law exhibited some flexibility as to those who could perform repairs. The consumer had to report the nonconformity to (1) the manufacturer, (2) one of its authorized dealers, or (3) the lessor.

The notice requirement ensured that the manufacturer learned of the problem. To take advantage of the law, the consumer then had to make the vehicle "available for repair," which obligated the manufacturer to repair the nonconformity.

The text of the statute simply did not state, as Thoroughbred urged, that the vehicle was "available for repair" only if it was actually taken to the manufacturer, authorized dealer, or lessor. The more flexible language, the court noted, preserved lemon law protection when the manufacturer directed the consumer to a repair shop other than the manufacturer's own authorized dealers, which could be few and far between.

Flexibility for repairs was also consistent with the law's broader legislative purpose of providing consumers with an alternative to the "inadequate, uncertain and expensive remedies" of the Uniform Commercial Code or the Magnuson–Moss Warranty Act. The lemon law was clearly remedial in nature, and the court reasoned that it should construe the statute "with a view towards the social problem which the legislature was addressing when enacting the law. "

Following this approach, the lemon law provided that "pecuniary loss" as used in the damages provision of the lemon law included the purchase price, not merely the costs flowing from the defect. "Certainly," the court said, "the law is intended to do more than simply parrot the remedies previously available to the consumer."

Under Thoroughbred's narrow interpretation, a consumer could lose the law's protections by taking the vehicle to a different repair facility even though directed to do so by the manufacturer. Such a result, the court noted, would be unjust to the point of absurdity, and the interpretation proposed by Thoroughbred would be an invitation to bad faith conduct by manufacturers.

In essence, Thoroughbred urged the court to find that Burzlaff lost his rights by following Thoroughbred's own instructions for repairing the vehicle. The text of the statute did not support that result, and it also raised serious, obvious issues of estoppel to avoid unjust results. The lemon law was enacted precisely because manufacturers could delay or avoid remedies through costly litigation over the precise language of a contractual warranty.

The lemon law thus protected consumers who went to a repair facility authorized by the manufacturer. This was true whether or not the facility was a "manufacturer's authorized motor vehicle dealer." The jury instructions in this case correctly distinguished the narrower requirements for notice (restricted to "the manufacturer or any authorized dealer") from the more flexible provision for repair at various facilities as long as the repairs were made on the manufacturer's behalf.

The jury instructions also focused on the central issue of the case: whether Amato Ford was acting on Thoroughbred's behalf when it was repairing Burzlaff's vehicle, or whether Burzlaff went there at his own risk and without Thoroughbred's authorization. The jury instructions explained accurately and clearly the issues relevant to the lemon law claim.

In the end, there was sufficient evidence to support the jury's verdict in favor of Burzlaff for his perpetually problematic motor trike.

18

Used Vehicles

PRACTICE POINTER

Under the explicit provisions of most lemon laws, *the term* "new motor vehicle" *includes "a demonstrator or lease–purchase vehicle as long as a manufacturer's warranty was issued as a condition of sale."*

The following case—*Chrysler v. Flowers*, 803 P.2d 314 (Wash. 1991)—shows that even in the absence of such language, a vehicle used by a manufacturer for field purposes before its sale to a consumer still qualifies as a "new motor vehicle" because it is a "demonstrator," is not titled before the consumer bought it under manufacturer's warranty, and is purchased within the statutory warranty period established by the lemon law.

In November 1986, Chrysler Motors transferred a new 1987 Dodge Ramcharger 4 x 4 to the company's zone office in Denver.

The Denver office subsequently assigned the SUV as a "field" vehicle to a Chrysler employee who used it for seven months for both business and personal use and drove it more than 20,000 miles. The automobile was never titled in Colorado.

Chrysler took the Ramcharger out of service as a field vehicle in July 1987 and then consigned it to an auction, which sold it on September 22 to Maria Flowers. At the time of her purchase, the odometer on the automobile read 23,410 miles. Chrysler issued a manufacturer's warranty that covered the first 24,000 miles of operation—in other words, with a mere 590 miles left.

Within a few days of the Ramcharger's purchase, serious problems with the vehicle began to surface, and Flowers immediately returned it to the dealer for repairs. The odometer read less than 24,000 miles at the time. The defective items included:

- Power steering,
- Transfer case,
- Drive train,
- Transmission,
- Windshield,
- Right turn signal,
- Brakes, and
- Excessive oil usage.

Flowers brought the Ramcharger to the dealer for repairs at least eight times, and it remained out of service for a total of 35 days.

The car was never satisfactorily repaired, and on July 11, 1988, Flowers submitted a request for arbitration under the lemon law. After a hearing on August 18, the arbitration board ordered Chrysler to repurchase the automobile, minus a reasonable offset for mileage.

Chrysler appealed, filing a motion for declaratory judgment that the automobile was a used vehicle not subject to the lemon law and that the consumer's claims should be dismissed. Flowers filed a cross motion for summary judgment seeking to enforce the arbitration board's decision.

The trial judge granted summary judgment to Flowers. The court ordered Chrysler to repurchase the automobile, as the arbitration panel had previously ordered, and also awarded attorneys' fees and costs to Flowers.

Chrysler appealed, and the question on appeal was a straightforward one: Does an automobile that has been driven extensively as a manufacturer's field vehicle qualify as a "new motor vehicle" under the lemon law?

The court concluded that the automobile in question did qualify as a new motor vehicle for the following reasons:

- It was a "demonstrator,"

- It was not titled before the consumer bought it under manufacturer's warranty, and
- It was purchased within the statutory warranty period established by the lemon law.

The state's lemon law explicitly addressed the purpose of the remedial legislation):

> The legislature recognizes that a new motor vehicle is a *major consumer purchase* and that a defective motor vehicle is likely to create *hardship* for, or may cause injury to, the consumer. The legislature further recognizes that *good cooperation and communication* between a manufacturer and a new motor vehicle dealer will considerably increase the likelihood that a new motor vehicle will be *repaired* within a reasonable number of attempts. (Emphasis added)

If such repair attempts failed, the lemon law created a mandatory arbitration panel to resolve disputes between manufacturers and dissatisfied consumers. The law provided relief from an unsafe or defective vehicle in the form of replacement or repurchase of the vehicle.

In enacting these measures, the state legislature made clear its intent to create the blend of private and public remedies necessary to induce manufacturers to improve quality control and to provide better warranty service for new motor vehicles. Thus, the court concluded, the lemon law applied only to *new* motor vehicles.

By the time the trial court entered its summary judgment order, the lemon law had been revised to define "new motor vehicle" as such:

> "New motor vehicle" means any new self-propelled vehicle primarily designed for the transportation of persons or property over the public highways that was leased or purchased in this state and registered in this state, but does not include vehicles purchased or leased by a business as part of a fleet of ten or more vehicles.
>
> If the motor vehicle is a motor home, this chapter shall apply to the self-propelled vehicle and chassis, but does not include those portions of the vehicle designated, used, or maintained primarily as a mobile dwelling, office, or commercial space. The term "new motor vehicle" does not include motorcycles or trucks

> with nineteen thousand pounds or more gross vehicle weight rating. *The term "new motor vehicle" includes a demonstrator or lease-purchase vehicle as long as a manufacturer's warranty was issued as a condition of sale.* (Emphasis added)

Thus, a demonstrator was now considered a new motor vehicle as long as a manufacturer's warranty was issued as a condition of sale. Unfortunately, the lemon law did not further define the terms *new* or *demonstrator.* Other statutory definitions in the statute, however, were helpful in defining the term *new motor vehicle.*

The lemon law defined a consumer as anyone who entered into an agreement for the transfer, lease, or purchase of a new motor vehicle, other than for resale or sublease, during the duration of the warranty period. Warranty period was defined as the period ending two years after the date of a new motor vehicle's delivery to a consumer, or the first 24,000 miles of operation, whichever occurred first. The court noted that it was necessary to bear these definitions in mind in defining a new motor vehicle, since every provision of an act had to be harmonized if possible.

Chrysler challenged the automobile's status both as "new" and as a "demonstrator," relying on the principle that undefined statutory terms should be given their ordinary meanings.

Flowers acknowledged that while a car with 23,000 miles might at first blush not seem new, she urged that remedial legislation such as the lemon law be broadly construed. It was Flowers's position that the automobile was new when she bought it because:

- It was a demonstrator and had never been previously titled or registered, and
- She bought the vehicle within both the manufacturer's warranty period and the lemon law warranty period.

The statutory warranty period ended two years after the delivery of a new motor vehicle to a consumer and covered the first 24,000 miles of operation. In the present case, Flowers bought the automobile when the mileage was less than 24,000 miles and thus subject to a new car warranty issued by the manufacturer.

Flowers argued that because she was the first party to register title to the automobile, and because she bought it within the statutory warranty period of the manufacturer and the statute, the automobile was new when she bought it. Her argument was bolstered by the court's conclusion that the automobile fit the definition of "demonstrator," which was considered a new car under the lemon law.

Furthermore, the "demonstrator" definition was approved by the state agency responsible for regulating manufacturers and dealers of new and used motor vehicles, including regulation of the use, registration, titling, and sale of "demonstrator" vehicles. The agency administrator provided the working definition of such vehicles:

> The term "demonstrator" or "demo" vehicle is a well-known and commonly used term in the automotive business and trade. The term is used to describe a vehicle used by the dealer/manufacturer which *has never been titled* and is being sold at retail to the public *for the first time*. (Emphasis added)

The category of "demonstrator" vehicle was created by special licensing and registration privileges granted to dealers and manufacturers. Special fees and excise taxes were levied, and dealers and manufacturers were granted the use of transferable dealer license plates.

Most "demonstrator" vehicles were not used exclusively for test driving vehicles by customers. Many states allowed "demonstrator" vehicles to be driven by spouses and employees. "Demonstrator" vehicles were thus commonly used for business and personal purposes even though technically the vehicle's use was to be connected with the dealer's and manufacturer's business operations and sales.

Deference to the administrative agency's construction of statutes, the court said, was appropriate within the agency's field of expertise. Furthermore, the definition was consistent with the state's licensing and auto-titling laws.

Under these circumstances, the court accepted the administrative definition of a "demonstrator" and concluded that the vehicle at issue fit within it. When Flowers purchased the car, it had been used only by the manufacturer, had never been titled, and was being sold at retail to the public for the first time.

The well-worn Ramcharger, it seemed, had suddenly sprung new life, and now it was a new motor vehicle under the lemon law statute.

19

Lease Cars

Practice Pointer

Lemon laws place obligations on both the lessor and the leasing company that must be satisfied to receive a refund. The statute is clear that *the leasing company, as holder of the title, must offer to transfer title in order to receive a refund.* In the absence of an offer, the manufacturer has no obligation to refund the current value of the lease to the leasing company.

In the case that follows—*Kilian v. Mercedes-Benz USA, LLC,* 799 N.W.2d 815 (Wis. 2010)—it is undisputed that the manufacturer did *not* receive an offer from the leasing company to transfer title until a lawsuit was filed. As a result, the manufacturer did not violate the lemon law, and the claim against it was properly dismissed.

A lessor's claim against the leasing company is typically based on a statutory provision that provides that "no person may enforce the lease against the consumer after the consumer receives a refund." The court assumed that the leasing company's phone calls and notices to the lessor informing him that he was in default of the lease agreement were in violation of this statutory provision as an attempt to enforce the lease after the lessor received his refund.

In March 2006, Steve Kilian leased a Mercedes-Benz under a 39-month lease assigned to the lessor, Daimler Financial Services. The automobile had numerous problems, and as a result, Kilian raised claims with Mercedes under the lemon law.

A little over a year later—on May 20, 2007—Kilian returned the vehicle to the dealership and received a refund check from Mercedes for the vehicle. The lease, not paid off, remained outstanding.

Predictably enough, Kilian then received phone calls from Daimler Financial indicating he was in default on the lease payments. Kilian also received a payment notice in the mail and a Federal Legal Notice, indicating that Daimler Financial would report negative information about Kilian's lease account to credit bureaus.

Kilian informed Daimler Financial that the vehicle had been returned to Mercedes and that the lease should be terminated. When Killian's efforts to resolve the matter failed, Kilian filed a lemon law suit against Mercedes on July 10. On August 29, Mercedes paid off the lease with a $95,252.37 payment to Daimler Financial.

In his lawsuit, Kilian claimed that Mercedes violated the lemon law by not automatically refunding to Daimler Financial the current value of the lease within 30 days of Kilian's demand for a refund. Mercedes maintained that its obligation to pay off the lease was only triggered when the lessor, Daimler Financial, offered to transfer title of the vehicle to Mercedes under the statute.

The lemon law delineated a manufacturer's obligation after reasonable attempts to repair a nonconformity failed. In the case of a leased vehicle, the statute required the manufacturer to:

> accept return of the motor vehicle, refund to the motor vehicle lessor and to any holder of a perfected security interest in the motor vehicle, as their interest may appear, the current value of the written lease and *refund to the consumer the amount the consumer paid under the written lease plus any sales tax and collateral costs, less a reasonable allowance for use.* (Emphasis added)

The lemon law then described how the consumer of a lemon was to seek the desired remedy. The consumer had to offer to transfer title to the vehicle to the manufacturer, and when the manufacturer provided a new motor vehicle or refund, the consumer then returned the lemon with the necessary title endorsements for the transfer of title.

A different procedure applied to a lessor of a lemon who did not have title to the vehicle. In that case, the lessee received a refund by offering to return the vehicle to the manufacturer, and when the refund was provided, the lessor returned the vehicle to the manufacturer.

The statute provided in regard to the consumer:

> To receive a refund due *the consumer shall offer to the manufacturer of the motor vehicle having the nonconformity to return that motor vehicle to that manufacturer.* No later than 30 days after that offer, the manufacturer shall provide the refund to the consumer. When the manufacturer provides the refund, *the consumer shall return the motor* vehicle having the nonconformity *to the manufacturer.* (Emphasis added)

The statute required the manufacturer to refund to the lessor the current value of the written lease, but the lemon law did not address how that refund was to be made.

Another statutory provision provided in regard to the lessor:

> To receive a refund . . . a motor vehicle *lessor shall offer to the manufacturer* of the motor vehicle having the nonconformity *to transfer title* of that motor vehicle *to that manufacturer.* No later than 30 days after that offer, the manufacturer shall provide the refund to the motor vehicle lessor. *When the manufacturer provides the refund,* the motor vehicle *lessor shall provide to the manufacturer the certificate of title* and all endorsements necessary to transfer title to the manufacturer. (Emphasis added)

Therefore, the lemon law statute placed obligations on both the consumer and the lessor that had to be satisfied to receive a refund. The leasing company, as holder of the title, had to offer to transfer title in order to receive its refund. The statute was unambiguous in this regard. In the absence of an offer by the leasing company, the manufacturer had *no* obligation to refund the current value of the lease to the leasing company.

In the present case, it was undisputed that Mercedes did *not* receive an offer from Daimler Financial to transfer title until sometime after this lawsuit was initiated. As a result, Mercedes did *not* violate the lemon law, and the claim against it was properly dismissed.

Kilian's claim against Daimler Financial was based on the statutory provision that "no person may enforce the lease against the consumer after the consumer receives a refund." The court assumed that Daimler

Financial's phone calls and notices to Kilian informing him that he was in default of the lease agreement were in violation of this statutory provision as an attempt to enforce the lease after Kilian received his refund.

Under the lemon law, a prevailing consumer was to be awarded twice the amount of any pecuniary loss, together with costs, disbursements, and reasonable attorney fees. The question that arose was what pecuniary loss did Kilian as a lessee suffer?

In his first itemization of damages, Kilian indicated that his damages were:

- His payments under the lease (less a reasonable use allowance) in the amount of $20,847.87, and
- The value of the written lease in the amount of $95,252.37.

Kilian doubled both figures and also claimed the accrual of actual attorney fees, costs, and prejudgment interest.

The trial court determined that Kilian was *not* allowed to recover those amounts, and Kilian filed a second itemization of damages that indicated he was entitled to recover:

- The sum of $5,478.36, which represented the amount Daimler Financial demanded as payment under the lease,
- The sum of $2,434.25, which represented Kilian's attorneys' fees incurred before filing the lawsuit, and
- The filing fee and service fees.

Kilian then doubled all of these sums.

Kilian also claimed he was entitled to seek "general damages" caused by Daimler Financial's negative reporting to credit bureaus, inconvenience damages, and equitable relief.

The trial court likewise determined that Kilian as a lessee was not entitled to these amounts.

On appeal, Kilian argued that his pre-suit attorney fees and costs, defamation general damages, and inconvenience damages were his pecuniary loss.

The appellate court held that attorneys' fees could not be awarded as pecuniary damages unless authorized by the statute or by a contract between the parties. The lemon law statute did not authorize an award of attorneys' fees as pecuniary damages, and lawsuit-related attorneys' fee were triggered only when the consumer prevailed in the litigation.

The court maintained that Kilian's claim for damages for the possible false reporting of default to credit bureaus failed because Kilian did not offer evidence that his credit was in fact injured by Daimler Financial's collection efforts.

The court concluded that Kilian's claim for inconvenience damages was too vague to be a valid element of damages, and his claim of emotional strain without physical injury was not compensable.

In other words, Kilian would receive no extraordinary compensation for his brief lease of a beautiful Mercedes-Benz that turned out to be a lemon.

20

Vehicle Return

PRACTICE POINTER

Lessees of new vehicles often discover warranty nonconformities in their vehicles early in the lease term and then return those vehicles to the leasing company.

Consumers who lease their vehicles are free to pursue their remedies under the lemon law, and any construction of the statute that absolutely bars recovery when the lessee no longer possesses the leased vehicle encourages manufacturers and dealers to promise to repair or correct any nonconformity in order to delay potential legal action until the lease is about to expire.

In the case that follows—*Singer v. Land Rover North America, Incorporated*, 955 F.Supp. 359 (N.J. 1997)—the manufacturer complied with the statutory elements of the lemon law because the vehicle was returned to the leasing company and resold.

The lessee argued that he should not lose his statutory remedy under the lemon law simply because he failed to extend the lease or otherwise retain the nonconforming vehicle.

The question is whether the statutory requirement contained in the lemon law—that a prevailing consumer receive a refund—is severable from the requirement that the manufacturer accept the return of the vehicle and thereby allow the lessee to seek a remedy even if the vehicle cannot be returned to the manufacturer.

Most lemon laws specifically afford relief to lessees, and the statutory period in which a lessee must seek repairs is often two years or 18,000 miles. A three- or four-year lease could easily expire before the final adjudication of a lemon lawsuit. To require the lessee in such circumstances to extend the lease term—or purchase the vehicle—would create a difficult hurdle for a potentially large class of lessees seeking protection of the law.

The statutory *requirement that a lemon had to be returned by the leasing company to the manufacturer is therefore not an indispensable part of the lemon law* as regards vehicle lessees.

On July 23, 1993, Evan Singer signed a lease with Chase Manhattan Bank for a new 1993 Range Rover sport utility vehicle. The term of the lease was 36 months, and the lease allowed 15,000 miles per year, or 45,000 miles over the entire term.

Singer periodically brought the Range Rover to the dealer and complained of poor handling and stalling, and Singer contended that these problems were never repaired. On April 26, 1996—after some 33 months of the lease (and nearing its end)—Singer filed suit.

Sometime at the end of July, Singer returned the vehicle to Chase Manhattan, and in early August, he informed Land Rover of the return. The SUV was inspected by a Land Rover representative on September 5, 1996, and shortly thereafter it was sold at auction.

Under the state's lemon law, manufacturers of new vehicles had to repair all defects that substantially impaired the vehicle's use, value, or safety if reported by the consumer or lessee within the first 18,000 miles of operation or within two years of delivery, whichever occurred first. A successful consumer under the statute was generally reimbursed the full purchase price of the car, less an allowance for reasonable use, plus the filing fees and other costs associated with bringing the action.

To comply with the law, the consumer had to return the defective vehicle to the manufacturer. Singer argued that New Jersey's lemon law provided only a "forced rescission" remedy to consumers, a remedy that would be unavailable to consumers who were unable to return the vehicle to the manufacturer.

Singer noted that no New Jersey cases addressed the status of a lessee who brought an action under the lemon law and subsequently returned the vehicle to the lessor before it was determined whether the vehicle was nonconforming.

The state lemon law specifically covered lease agreements. The statute provided:

> A consumer *who leases a new motor vehicle shall have the same remedies against a manufacturer under this section as a consumer* who purchases a new motor vehicle. If it is determined that the lessee is entitled to a refund, the consumer shall return the leased vehicle to the lessor or manufacturer, the consumer's lease agreement with the motor vehicle lessor shall be terminated, and no penalty for early termination shall be assessed.
>
> *The manufacturer shall provide the consumer with a full refund of the amount actually paid by the consumer under the lease agreement*, including any additional charges if actually paid by the consumer, less a reasonable allowance for vehicle use. The manufacturer shall provide the motor vehicle lessor with a full refund of the vehicle's original purchase price plus any unrecovered interest expense, less the amount actually paid by the consumer under the agreement. Refunds shall be made to the lessor and lienholder, if any, as their interests appear on the records of ownership maintained by the Director of the Division of Motor Vehicles. (Emphasis added)

Singer pointed out that the lemon law granted lessees the "same remedies" as buyers. The remedial scheme included the consumer's return of the vehicle, to either the manufacturer or the lessor. Clearly, the statute anticipated that the consumer would be in possession of the vehicle at the time that it was judged to be a lemon.

The lemon law also provided that the lessor return the car to the manufacturer and be made whole. The transaction between lessor and manufacturer was a prerequisite to the further requirement of the statute—that the manufacturer include a warning that the vehicle was returned as a lemon, in the event the vehicle was re-sold or re-leased.

Although the plain language of the statute reflected the legislature's assumption that the lemon be returned to the manufacturer, it could not be said that the law was intended to protect lessors. In fact, lessors were specifically excluded from the statutory definition of "consumers."

Land Rover placed great importance on the twin requirements that:

- The lessor be made whole by the manufacturer, and
- That any future buyer be warned that the vehicle has been returned to the manufacturer as a lemon.

In the present case, Land Rover clearly complied with those statutory elements because the vehicle had already been returned to the lessor and resold.

Singer argued that he should not lose his statutory remedy under the lemon law simply because he failed to extend the lease or otherwise retain the nonconforming vehicle.

The question for the court was whether the statutory requirement contained in the lemon law—that a prevailing consumer receive a refund—was severable from the requirement that the manufacturer accept the return of the vehicle, and thereby allow the consumer to seek a remedy even if the vehicle could not be returned to the manufacturer.

The purpose of the lemon law, the court noted, was to provide "procedures to expeditiously resolve disputes between a consumer and a manufacturer" without requiring the consumer to prove fraud. Clearly, the lemon law was a remedial statute, and the courts were to construe it so as to achieve its overall purpose.

The lemon law specifically afforded relief to lessees, and the statutory period in which a lessee must seek repairs was two years or 18,000 miles. A three- or four-year lease could easily expire before the final adjudication of a lemon lawsuit. To require the lessee in such circumstances to extend the lease term—or purchase the vehicle—would create a difficult hurdle for a potentially large class of consumers seeking protection of the law.

The court reasoned that although many consumers would no doubt discover nonconformities in their vehicles early in the lease term, any construction of the lemon law that barred recovery when the consumer no longer possessed the leased vehicle could encourage manufacturers and dealers to promise to repair a nonconformity in order to delay legal action until the lease expired.

It was, the court stated, the lemon law's stated aim to "expeditiously resolve disputes." The statute had to be construed so as to promote cooperative resolution of disputes in a manner that would not encourage delay. The court concluded that the statutory requirement that the lessor has to return a lemon to the manufacturer was *not* an indispensable part of the lemon law.

For all of these reasons, Land Rover's motion for partial summary judgment was soundly denied.

21

Demonstrators

PRACTICE POINTER

The phrase "comparable new motor vehicle" in the lemon law is admittedly ambiguous as it concerns "demonstrator" vehicles, but the courts invariably permit the replacement of a nonconforming demonstrator with a comparable demonstrator.

In the case that follows—*Dussault v. Chrysler Corporation*, 600 N.W.2d 6 (Wis. 1999)—the consumer asked the court to adopt a different definition, contending that "comparable new motor vehicle" did not include demonstrators and that "new" meant "new."

The courts are generally satisfied that a manufacturer has fulfilled its obligation by offering to replace the consumer's lemon with a vehicle that places the consumer in the same position and that *a manufacturer satisfies its obligation by replacing a nonconforming demonstrator with a late-model demonstrator with comparable features.*

On July 10, 1995, Michele Dussault purchased a 1994 Eagle Vision from a Chrysler dealership in Burlington, Wisconsin. Dussault purchased the car as a demonstrator with 6,302 miles on the odometer.

Within the first year of ownership, Dussault experienced at least one warranty nonconformity that was not successfully repaired by the dealer.

A little more than two years after the car's purchase—in a letter dated September 9, 1997—Dussault notified Chrysler that the vehicle was a lemon; she demanded that Chrysler accept its return and provide a "comparable new motor vehicle" and collateral costs connected with repairing the vehicle.

In October, Chrysler responded that it had a comparable "new demo" for Dussault.

The "comparable" vehicle was a 1997 Eagle Vision with 5,728 miles—in other words, a vehicle three years *newer* and with 574 *fewer* miles. Dussault was not pleased with the replacement, and she said she would not accept a "new" demo because the lemon law required a "comparable new motor vehicle," *not* a demonstrator. Chrysler responded that the term *comparable new motor vehicle* included a replacement demonstrator that was comparable to Dussault's present demonstrator model.

On October 13, 1997, Dussault filed suit against Chrysler. Her first claim sought "the choice of either a comparable new motor vehicle or rescission of the afore-described purchase agreement, and the refund of all the monies," and the second claim alleged damages due to Chrysler's failure to repair.

The first issue presented to the court was whether a manufacturer fulfilled its obligation to provide a "comparable new motor vehicle" under the statute by offering to replace a consumer's nonconforming demonstrator vehicle with another demonstrator.

The court admitted that the phrase "comparable new motor vehicle" was somewhat ambiguous, but because the purpose of the statute was to put a consumer in the same position the consumer was in at the time the vehicle was purchased, the court concluded that the lemon law envisioned the replacement of a nonconforming demonstrator with a comparable demonstrator.

The second issue was whether a consumer could pursue an alternative remedy under the statute once the consumer had established that the manufacturer was provided a "reasonable attempt to repair" the nonconforming vehicle. The court concluded that when a "reasonable attempt to repair" was demonstrated, the consumer was limited to the remedies under the lemon law.

In November 1997, Chrysler filed a motion for summary judgment, claiming that it had fully complied with the lemon law by making a replacement vehicle available. Dussault reiterated that Chrysler was responsible for a comparable *new* motor vehicle, not a comparable *demonstrator* vehicle. The trial court agreed that Chrysler had complied with the lemon law, and it dismissed Dussault's claims.

The issues raised on appeal involved the statutory interpretation of the lemon law statute. In construing ambiguous language, the court examined the history, context, subject matter, scope, and object of the statute.

The language "comparable new motor vehicle" in the statute provided:

(1) If after a reasonable attempt to repair the nonconformity is not repaired, the manufacturer shall . . .

(2) At the direction of a consumer . . .

> Accept return of the motor vehicle and *replace the motor vehicle with a comparable new motor vehicle* and refund any collateral costs. (Emphasis added)

Dussault contended that Chrysler failed to comply with the statute in providing a 1997 demonstrator to replace her 1994 demonstrator. Dussault urged the court to read the phrase "comparable new motor vehicle" as meaning a comparable "brand-new" motor vehicle. Dussault asserted that the term *new* in the phrase "comparable new motor vehicle" cannot refer to a demonstrator because a demonstrator was by definition a "used" vehicle.

Chrysler countered that because a "motor vehicle" included a demonstrator, a "comparable new motor vehicle" also included a demonstrator. Chrysler asserted that Dussault's reading of the statute would render the term *comparable* meaningless because a used demonstrator—such as Dussault's vehicle—was not comparable to a brand-new vehicle.

Chrysler claimed that an ambiguity existed in the plain meaning of the phrase "comparable new motor vehicle," and therefore the court must look to the purpose of the lemon law, which was "to return the purchaser of a lemon to the position he or she was in at the time the vehicle was purchased."

The court first addressed Dussault's argument that the plain language of the statute did not contemplate a demonstrator. In order for Dussault to make a claim under statute, Dussault had to follow its requirements, which provided:

> If a *new motor vehicle* does not conform to an applicable express warranty and the consumer reports the nonconformity to the manufacturer, the motor vehicle lessor or any of the manufacturer's authorized motor vehicle dealers and makes the motor vehicle available for repair before the expiration of the warranty or one year

> after first delivery of the motor vehicle to a consumer, whichever is sooner, the nonconformity shall be repaired. (Emphasis added)

Neither party disputed that the phrase "new motor vehicle" in the statute applied to Dussault's 1994 demonstrator. Dussault asserted, and Chrysler acknowledged, that the demonstrator's nonconformities had to be repaired.

Dussault, however, asked the court to adopt a different definition of "new motor vehicle." She contended that "comparable new motor vehicle" did not include a demonstrator and that because "new" meant "new," it could not by definition include a used car like a demonstrator.

In construing the meaning of "comparable new motor vehicle," the court first considered the definition of the term *motor vehicle*, which included "any motor driven vehicle required to be registered . . . including a demonstrator or executive vehicle not titled or titled by a manufacturer or a motor vehicle dealer, which a consumer purchases or accepts transfer of in this state."

The court next examined the terms *comparable* and *new*, neither of which was defined or mentioned in the definition of the term *motor vehicle*. The court read the term *comparable* to mean a similar model vehicle with similar features, such as the type of engine, transmission, brakes, seat upholstery, and accessories.

As for the word "new," Dussault pointed out that a "new" motor vehicle was defined as "any untitled or non-privately titled motor vehicle of the stated model year which has not been a demonstrator." The court was not convinced that this definition applied to the lemon law.

The court noted that reasonable persons could differ as to the meaning of the phrase "comparable new motor vehicle." Because the definition of the term *motor vehicle* included a demonstrator that was not titled, the court was uncertain about what the term *new* added to the term:

- If "new" meant "not titled," then "new" would be superfluous,
- If "new" meant "brand new," then demonstrators would be excluded, and
- If "new" meant vehicles "before the expiration of the warranty or one year after first delivery of the motor vehicle to a consumer, whichever is sooner," then demonstrators, "brand-new" vehicles, and previously owned vehicles would be covered.

Because the meaning of "new" was unclear, the court concluded that "comparable new motor vehicle" was simply ambiguous.

In order to reconcile this ambiguity, the court considered the purpose of the lemon law—to improve auto manufacturers' quality control and reduce the inconvenience, expense, frustration, fear, and emotional trauma that lemon owners endure.

More importantly, the lemon law sought "to provide an incentive for a manufacturer to put the purchaser of a new car back to the position the purchaser thought they were in at the time they bought the car."

When Dussault first purchased her 1994 Eagle Vision in July 1995, the vehicle was a demonstrator with 6,302 miles, six-cylinder engine, automatic transmission, leather seats, and a suggested retail price of $25,787.

In October 1997, Chrysler offered to replace Dussault's vehicle with a 1997 Eagle Vision demonstrator with 5,728 miles, six-cylinder engine, automatic transmission, leather seats, and a suggested retail price of $26,290.

The replacement vehicle had similar features as the original vehicle, the only significant difference being that the replacement was three years *newer* than the original vehicle.

The court was therefore satisfied that Chrysler had fulfilled its obligation by offering to replace Dussault's lemon with a vehicle that put her in the same position she was in at the time she purchased the original car and that a manufacturer satisfied its obligation to provide a "comparable new motor vehicle" by replacing a nonconforming demonstrator with a late-model demonstrator with comparable features.

The trial court's dismissal of Dussault's lemon law claims was thus affirmed, and Ms. Dussault would, sadly enough, be relegated to driving the Eagle Vision—the newer car with fewer miles.

22

Motor Homes

Practice Pointer

The addition of the term *passenger* to the definition of motor vehicle in the lemon law simply means that the vehicle is designed for and capable of carrying persons other than the driver. *Nothing in the statute suggests that the legislature intended to limit the term to automobiles or other specific type of motor vehicle, including motor homes.*

Most lemon laws provide for an award of triple damages to a successful consumer if the manufacturer either does not act in good faith in the informal dispute settlement procedure or had not established such a procedure.

In the case that follows—*Sweeney v. SMC Corporation*, 37 P.3d 244 (Or. 2002)—the manufacturer argued that the lemon law statute limited the consumer's remedy if the consumer pursued other judicial remedies as well and that when a consumer pursued other claims, the lemon law remedy was limited to the refund of the purchase price of the vehicle, together with reimbursement of certain other costs and fees authorized by the lemon law. Any recovery for triple damages under the lemon law was a recovery in excess of what the statute authorized.

The courts hold that in the case of a manufacturer that did not have an informal dispute settlement procedure in place which would have prevented triple damages limited to a successful consumer, *the lemon law statute did not preclude an award of triple damages based on the manufacturer's failure to have established an informal dispute settlement procedure.*

It made sense to read the statute as limiting the consumer's remedy to refund or replace the defective vehicle, but not as precluding a triple damage award for the manufacturer's failure to provide a good-faith informal dispute settlement procedure. To deny triple damages would frustrate the purpose of giving an independent incentive to manufacturers to provide a settlement procedure; it would provide manufacturers with a windfall in that sense.

In 1996, William and Susan Sweeney bought a motor home from SMC Corporation for the sum of $188,000.

Soon afterward the Sweeneys discovered a number of defects in the vehicle, both in its mechanical operation and in its living facilities. Among other things, the Sweeneys complained about the steering, transmission, air conditioning, appliances, water pressure, and a chemical odor that caused nose and eye irritation, breathing difficulties, and headaches.

The Sweeneys attempted to have these significant problems with the motor home fixed, but the repairs were never to their satisfaction. During its first five months, the motor home spent more than 120 days—four months!—in the shop.

The Sweeneys eventually filed a lawsuit against SMC, asserting a claim under the lemon law together with claims for breach of express and implied warranties under both state and federal law. Before trial, SMC moved for partial summary judgment on the ground that the lemon law did not apply to motor homes. The trial court denied the motion.

At trial, the jury awarded the Sweeneys damages under the lemon law consisting of the purchase price of $188,000, along with $14,000 for taxes, license, and registration fees. The jury also awarded the Sweeneys an identical amount—that is, $188,000—on their warranty claims.

In accordance with the lemon law statute, the court tripled the lemon law damages and entered judgment for $606,000, along with attorneys' fees, costs, and disbursements. Because the verdict under the warranty claims duplicated the purchase price refund under the lemon law, the court did not separately enter judgment for that amount.

On appeal, SMC first renewed its position that the lemon law did not apply to motor homes, arguing that a motor home did not meet the law's definition of "motor vehicle."

The lemon law statute defined motor vehicle as a passenger motor vehicle, which unfortunately was not defined. Only the term *motor vehicle* was defined, and it was generally described as "a vehicle that is self-propelled or designed for self-propulsion."

This case therefore turned on the significance of the legislature's choice to add the term *passenger* to the term *motor vehicle* in the lemon law. The court held that the common characteristic of vehicles that are passenger motor vehicles is that they have the design and capacity to carry persons other than the driver.

Nothing in the lemon law suggested that the legislature intended to limit the term to automobiles or to other specific types of motor vehicle. The court reasoned that by expressly covering *all* motor vehicles—modified only by the adjective "passenger"—the statutory text plainly encompassed any and all motor vehicles that were designed for, and capable of, carrying passengers other than the driver.

SMC, on the other hand, argued that because the legislature defined "passenger motor vehicle" by reference to a statute that defined only "motor vehicle," it intended to restrict the kinds of motor vehicles that were subject to the lemon law. By way of example, SMC referred to a number of other definitions in the motor vehicle code that defined more limited classes of motor vehicles, such as farm tractors, golf carts, and military tanks.

SMC pointed out that in defining motor vehicles for purposes of the lemon law, the legislature chose to use only the general definition of motor vehicle. That fact, suggested SMC, was evidence that the legislature no more intended to include motor homes in the lemon law than other types of motor vehicles such as farm tractors, golf carts, and military tanks.

SMC also noted that the statute separately defined "motor home" as a motor vehicle that is "reconstructed, permanently altered or originally designed to provide facilities for human habitation." SMC argued that by this separate definition, the legislature intended to *exclude* any separately defined type of motor vehicle, including motor homes, from being a passenger motor vehicle under the lemon law.

Finally, relying on the ordinary meaning of passenger as someone who rode in an automobile, SMC contended that a passenger motor vehicle must be a motor vehicle that is primarily designed for transportation, not for habitation. Therefore, because the statute defined a motor home as a vehicle designed to provide human habitation, a motor home could not be a passenger motor vehicle, reasoned SMC.

The court held that SMC's argument failed in at least two respects. First, "motor vehicle" was defined in the statute as a broad category that included every vehicle that was "self-propelled or designed for self-propulsion." The more specific classes of vehicles to which SMC referred were all initially defined as motor vehicles. Those definitions then differentiated each class by describing the particular characteristics that set the class apart from other types of motor vehicles.

In other words, the specific definitions in the statute were subsets of the general category of motor vehicles, and these definitions did not limit the scope of vehicles the general category encompassed. Thus, the legislature defined "motor vehicle" in the lemon law by expressly referring to the general definition of motor vehicle in the statute and by adding the modifier "passenger" to it.

The court concluded that the legislature therefore intended the term *motor vehicle* to mean *any* type of motor vehicle, provided that the vehicle was also a passenger motor vehicle.

The second problem with SMC's argument, said the court, was its assumption that a motor vehicle that contained certain characteristics—such as being adapted for human habitation—could also feature other characteristics—such as being adapted for carrying passengers. Assuming that the definition of motor home in the statute was relevant, nothing in that definition prevented a motor home from also being a passenger motor vehicle.

Again, the statute defined motor home as a motor vehicle that was "reconstructed, permanently altered or originally designed to provide facilities for human habitation." Those characteristics did not necessarily preclude a motor home from having other characteristics in common with other motor vehicles, such as the ability to carry passengers. Nothing in the statutory provisions indicated that a motor home could *not* be a motor vehicle.

The history of amendments to the lemon law reinforced this conclusion, the court said. As originally adopted, the definition of motor vehicle in the statute concluded with the phrase "other than a motorcycle." In order to exempt motorcycles from the law's coverage, the legislature expressly excluded them. In 1989, the legislature repealed the express exclusion, which had the effect of bringing motorcycles back into the lemon law.

The initial adoption, and the later repeal, of the exemption for motorcycles suggested that the legislature understood the reference in the statute to passenger motor vehicle to encompass motor vehicles other than automobiles that were designed for and capable of transporting passengers unless such vehicles were expressly exempted. That was true even though a motorcycle was a subclass of motor vehicles that, like a motor home, was separately defined in the vehicle code.

Moreover, a motorcycle was described as having, among other characteristics, a "seat or saddle for use of the rider," and the definition said nothing about a motorcycle's capacity to carry passengers.

Many different kinds of motor vehicles qualified as being designed for and having the capacity to carry passengers. A motor home was included in that category. In the mind of the court, the fact that a motor home also provided habitation was irrelevant to that conclusion. A vehicle that was capable of fulfilling one function was not necessarily incapable of fulfilling another.

SMC did not dispute that the motor home in question was designed for carrying more than one person, only one of whom would be driving at any particular time. Any person who was not driving would necessarily be a passenger. The Sweeneys' motor home was thus a passenger motor vehicle.

SMC argued that such an interpretation of "passenger motor vehicle" would result in the lemon law being applied to transactions beyond what the legislature intended. But that argument overlooked the fact that the range of claims coming within the lemon law was not dictated solely by what qualified as a new passenger motor vehicle. Only a "consumer" was entitled to a remedy under the lemon law, and a "consumer" was defined as the "purchaser or lessee, other than for purposes of resale, of a new motor vehicle normally used for personal, family, or household purposes."

As a result, the normal use of the vehicle and the consumer's purpose were significant limitations on the availability of a lemon law remedy. In this case, there was no dispute that the motor home was being used for personal, family, or household purposes or that the Sweeneys purchased their motor home other than for the purpose of resale.

For all of the above reasons, the appellate court affirmed the denial of SMC's motion for partial summary judgment.

In its second assignment of error, SMC argued that the trial court erred by trebling the amount of the jury's verdict pursuant to the statute when it entered judgment. SMC contended that, because the Sweeneys pursued other judicial remedies in addition to a lemon law claim, the statute limited a consumer's recovery to the purchase price of the vehicle and certain incidental expenses, and thus the statute precluded an award of triple damages based on that refunded purchase price.

Under the lemon law, a consumer was entitled to a remedy if:

- The new motor vehicle did not conform to the manufacturer's warranties,
- The consumer reported the nonconformities to the manufacturer or dealer within a specified period, and
- The manufacturer was notified of the defects and had an opportunity to correct them.

A consumer was entitled to one of two remedies if the failure to repair or correct defects under the warranty impaired the vehicle's use, market value, or safety.

First, the manufacturer could be required to replace the motor vehicle with a new one. Or, alternatively, it could be required to accept return of the vehicle from the consumer and to refund the purchase price and certain associated costs, less a "reasonable allowance" for the consumer's use of the vehicle.

The remedy available under the lemon law was not exclusive, and it was not intended "in any way to limit the rights or remedies that are otherwise available to a consumer under any other law." But neither could the lemon law be used in conjunction with other remedies to recover more than the lemon law alone would provide.

The original act encouraged manufacturers to establish informal dispute settlement procedures in accordance with applicable federal regulations. If a manufacturer did so, the consumer could not seek a remedy under the lemon law without first resorting to the procedure.

The legislature later amended the lemon law to increase the incentives to manufacturers to provide informal dispute settlement procedures and to ensure that the procedures functioned fairly. Consumers were required to notify a manufacturer and give it an opportunity to correct defects before seeking a remedy under the lemon law, and "notification" included a request for an informal dispute resolution procedure.

The current statute provided for an award of triple damages to a successful plaintiff if the manufacturer either did not act in good faith in the informal dispute settlement procedure or had not established such a procedure. In both cases, a successful plaintiff would also be entitled to attorney fees and costs.

With that background, the court turned to SMC's challenge to the award of triple damages in this case. SMC's argument depended on the language of the statute that limited the consumer's remedy if the consumer pursued other judicial remedies in addition to a lemon law claim.

In a relevant part, the statute provided:

> If the consumer *elects to pursue any other remedy* in state or federal court, the remedy available [under the lemon law] *shall not be available insofar as it would result in recovery in excess of the recovery authorized* by [the lemon law] without proof of fault resulting in damages in excess of such recovery. (Emphasis added)

In this case, the Sweeneys succeeded on claims brought under state and federal law that were additional to their remedy under the lemon law. SMC argued that, because the Sweeneys pursued those other claims, their lemon law remedy was limited to the refund of the purchase price of the vehicle, together with reimbursement of certain other costs and fees, as authorized by the lemon law.

According to SMC, any recovery for triple damages under the lemon law was a recovery in excess of what the statute authorized and therefore required proof of fault, which the Sweeneys did not present.

The court held that if a consumer pursued other judicial remedies in addition to a lemon law claim, the lemon law statute limited the consumer's remedy for purchase of a defective vehicle. The lemon law, said the court, did not preclude an award for the manufacturer's failure to have a good-faith informal dispute settlement procedure in place.

The purpose of the limitation provision in the lemon law was to prevent a windfall to a plaintiff in the form of a double recovery for the value of the defective vehicle. In contrast, the triple damages award served a different purpose—penalizing manufacturers who failed to have in place a good-faith informal dispute settlement procedure.

In the context of the lemon law as a whole, then, it made sense to read the statute as limiting only the consumer's remedy for refund or replacement of the defective vehicle and not as also precluding a triple award for the manufacturer's failure to provide a good-faith informal dispute settlement procedure.

To deny a triple damages award because the consumer pursued multiple potential remedies for the defective vehicle would do nothing to further the purpose of avoiding a double recovery by a successful plaintiff. It would, however, frustrate the purpose of providing an independent incentive to manufacturers to provide a settlement procedure, and it would provide manufacturers with a windfall in that sense. For that reason, SMC's proposed understanding of the key statutory language simply is not plausible when considered in the context of the statutory scheme as a whole.

Consequently, the court held that when a consumer pursued other judicial remedies in addition to a lemon law claim, the statute limited only a consumer's remedy under the statute for the failure to conform the motor vehicle to its express warranties.

The lemon law statute did not preclude an award of triple damages based on the manufacturer's failure to have established a good-faith informal dispute settlement procedure. Therefore, in this case, the trial court did not err in awarding triple damages to the Sweeneys because it was undisputed that the manufacturer had no such procedure in place.

The trial court's decision was thus affirmed, and the Sweeneys went away from the courthouse with a very large check for all the trouble they endured with their beloved motor home.

23

Motorcycles

Practice Pointer

The phrase "passenger motor vehicle" in the lemon law has been held to apply only to automobiles (and larger versions thereof) and *not* motorcycles, unless explicitly included.

In the case that follows—*Cagiva North America, Inc. v. Schenk*, 239 Conn. 1 (1996)—the court reasoned that reading the general statutes as a whole strongly suggests that *motorcycles were not passenger motor vehicles*. First, the statute contained an explicit definition of "motorcycle," and including motorcycles in the class of passenger motor vehicles would be redundant. Second, no definition in the statute expressly refers solely to automobiles. The only definition that implicitly fills this role was that of passenger motor vehicle.

Other motor vehicle statutes indicate that the legislature uses the phrase *passenger motor vehicle* to refer specifically to automobiles, while it used the term *motorcycle* to refer to motorcycles. One statute governs fees for passenger motor vehicles, while another governs fees for motorcycles. The statute requiring two sets of safety belts refers only to passenger motor vehicles and clearly does not include motorcycles.

The legislative history also supports the conclusion that the phrase *passenger motor vehicles* includes only what were commonly thought of as automobiles and larger versions like station wagons and vans, but not motorcycles. The committee hearings regarding the proposed lemon law all involve defective cars, and at no time during the house proceedings were motorcycles, or any vehicles other than cars, mentioned.

Given the language, purpose, and legislative history of the lemon law, the courts are generally not persuaded that the statute's remedial purpose is broad enough to include motorcycles.

A company known as Cagiva was the exclusive importer and wholesale distributor in the United States for the expensive line of Ducati motorcycles manufactured in Italy. On May 16, 1992, Edward Schenk purchased a new Ducati motorcycle from a dealer in Norwalk, Connecticut.

Over the next several years, Schenk experienced repeated mechanical problems with the vehicle.

In 1995—some three years after its purchase—Schenk initiated compulsory arbitration proceedings against Cagiva pursuant to the state's lemon law. The dispositive issue was whether a motorcycle was a passenger motor vehicle within the meaning of the statute.

Cagiva argued that claims regarding motorcycles were not covered by the lemon law and, therefore, could not be required to arbitrate Schenk's claim. The arbitration panel rejected this contention, and after a hearing, the trial court rendered a decision in favor of Schenk.

On appeal, Cagiva claimed that the trial court improperly concluded that a motorcycle was a passenger motor vehicle within the meaning of the statute. The appellate court agreed.

The court pointed out that the lemon law was a remedial statute that protected purchasers of new passenger motor vehicles. The statute was designed to compel manufacturers of passenger motor vehicles to fulfill the obligations of express warranties to their consumers and to facilitate a consumer's recovery against the manufacturer of a defective vehicle should a dispute arise.

The lemon law directed that "if a new motor vehicle does not conform to all applicable express warranties, and the consumer reports the nonconformity to the manufacturer during the period of two years following the date of original delivery of the motor vehicle to a consumer or during the period of the first eighteen thousand miles of operation, whichever period ends first, the manufacturer shall make such repairs as are necessary to conform the vehicle to such express warranties."

The lemon law also established an arbitration procedure for consumer disputes with manufacturers over warranties. If the arbitration panel found that the manufacturer failed to meet its obligations, the statute authorized a number of remedies, including a refund of the purchase price.

Whether a motorcycle was a passenger motor vehicle for the purposes of the statute was a question of statutory interpretation.

In seeking to discern legislative intent, the court looked to the words of the statute, the legislative history, the legislative policy, and the statute's relationship to existing legislation and common law principles governing the same general subject matter.

Cagiva's primary claim was that the state department of consumer protection lacked the authority under the lemon law to compel arbitration regarding motorcycles because a motorcycle was not a passenger motor vehicle as defined in the relevant statutes.

Cagiva also asserted that the definition of passenger motor vehicle clearly excluded motorcycles and was limited to the class of vehicles commonly known as "automobiles."

The Department of Consumer Protection, however, did not contend that a motorcycle was a passenger motor vehicle, but rather that the definition ought to be liberally construed in light of the objectives of the remedial statute.

After much analysis, the court concluded for the purposes of the lemon law that the phrase *passenger motor vehicle* referred only to automobiles and its larger versions.

The court began its discussion with the statutory definitions for motor vehicle and passenger motor vehicle. Although the definition of motor vehicle was broad enough to include motorcycles, the addition of the word "passenger," the court said, suggested that the legislature intended to limit the scope of that phrase.

The court reasoned that reading the general statutes as a whole strongly suggested that motorcycles were not passenger motor vehicles. First, the statute contained an explicit definition of "motorcycle." Including motorcycles in the class of passenger motor vehicles would be redundant. Second, no definition in the statute expressly referred only to automobiles. The only definition that implicitly filled this role was that of the passenger motor vehicle.

Other motor vehicle statutes indicated that the legislature used the phrase *passenger motor vehicle* to refer specifically to automobiles, while it used the term *motorcycle* to refer to motorcycles.

For example, one statute governed fees for passenger motor vehicles, while another governed fees for motorcycles. The statute requiring two sets of safety belts referred only to passenger motor vehicles and clearly did not include motorcycles.

The legislative history of the lemon law also supported the conclusion that the phrase *passenger motor vehicles* included only what were commonly thought of as automobiles and larger versions such as station wagons and vans, but not motorcycles. The committee hearings regarding the proposed lemon law all involved defective cars. At no time during the house proceedings were motorcycles, or any vehicles other than cars, mentioned.

It was true, as the Department of Consumer Protection argued, that the lemon law was a remedial statute that should be read broadly in favor of those consumers whom the law was designed to protect. But that general principle merely begged the question of which consumers the lemon law was, in fact, designed to protect.

The court agreed that the law should be read broadly in favor of automobile consumers, but that given the language, purpose, and legislative history of the lemon law, the court was not persuaded that its remedial purpose was broad enough to include motorcycles.

The court concluded, then, that a motorcycle was *not* a *passenger* motor vehicle within the meaning of the lemon law—no matter how many people could sit on it!

24

Personal Injury Recovery

Practice Pointer

Lemon laws typically *do not allow consumers to seek personal injury damages* for a violation of the statute, and the courts have held that to hold otherwise would *impermissibly expand the scope of the statute.*

In the case that follows—*Gosse v. Navistar International Transportation Company*, 605 N.W.2d 896 (Wis.1999)—the court concludes that the words "any damages" in the statute are ambiguous. Reasonable minds might disagree as to whether the legislature intended to allow a consumer to recover personal injury damages, but in light of its statutory purpose, allowing the recovery of personal injury damages is contrary to the purpose of the law.

The lemon law is enacted to give consumers a means by which to ensure that a newly purchased vehicle will conform to its warranty. Allowing a consumer to seek personal injury damages does not further that purpose, and to interpret the statute as such would impermissibly expand its scope.

On February 1, 1995, Robert Gosse entered into a lease agreement for a new International Tractor truck, which was manufactured by Navistar International Transportation Corporation. About two months later,

Gosse brought the truck to an authorized dealer, complaining that it vibrated excessively when operating under a full load. The dealer was unable to repair the problem.

Gosse returned the truck to the dealer repeatedly over the next year, but the dealer was unable to correct the problem. About a year and a half later—on July 8, 1996—Gosse wrote to the manufacturer Navistar, asserting that his truck was a lemon and requesting Navistar to either repair the truck or allow him to return it for a refund.

Navistar replied, explaining that the vibration for this type of truck was normal, and so the company declined to make any financial concessions.

Gosse eventually filed suit against Navistar for violation of the state lemon law on the grounds that the vibrations impaired the truck's use, value, and safety. Gosse asserted that the vibrations ruined the truck's value and that the vibrations caused injuries to his hands when he operated the truck.

At the final pretrial conference, the trial court ruled that Gosse could not seek personal injury damages based on the lemon law.

On appeal, Gosse asserted that the lemon law statute explicitly allowed a consumer to recover personal injury damages:

> In addition to pursuing any other remedy, a consumer *may bring an action to recover for any damages caused by a violation of this section*. The court shall award a consumer who prevails in such an action twice the amount of any pecuniary loss, together with costs, disbursements and reasonable attorney fees, and any equitable relief the court determines appropriate. (Emphasis added)

Gosse pointed out that the legislature amended the statute to include the language "may bring an action to recover for any damages caused" by a violation of this section.

By using the words "any damages," Gosse contended, the legislature intended to allow consumers to recover for *all* damages that might be linked to a violation of the lemon law, including personal injury damages.

After careful analysis, the court concluded that the words "any damages" in the statute were ambiguous. Reasonable people, the court said, might disagree as to whether, by using the words "any damages," the legislature intended to allow a consumer to recover personal injury damages. Thus, the court interpreted the language of the statute within the context of its purpose.

Under the lemon law, if a motor vehicle does not conform to its express warranty, the nonconformity must be repaired if the consumer makes the vehicle available for repair before the warranty expired or within one year after the vehicle was delivered to the consumer. If the nonconformity could not be repaired, the manufacturer had to accept the return of the vehicle and replace it or provide a refund. The lemon law was violated when the manufacturer failed to voluntarily replace or repurchase the lemon vehicle within 30 days after receipt of the consumer's demand under the statute, and the consumer was allowed to enforce the statute by bringing legal action.

In light of this statutory purpose, the court concluded that allowing the recovery of personal injury damages was contrary to the purpose of the law. The lemon law, the court pointed out, was enacted to deal with warranty disputes between manufacturers and consumers, and it sought to provide an incentive to the manufacturer to promptly restore unfortunate consumers back to where they were when they first purchased that new automobile.

The lemon law was enacted to give consumers a means by which to ensure that a newly purchased vehicle would conform to its warranty. Allowing a consumer to seek personal injury damages did not further that purpose, and to interpret the statute as such would impermissibly expand its scope.

The court pointed out, however, that Gosse was not precluded from asserting a second claim under another law to recover damages for personal injuries caused by a defective truck.

Alas, the adjudication of Gosse's nagging hand injuries would have to wait for resolution another day.

25

Informal Dispute Resolution

PRACTICE POINTER

Under the lemon law, a manufacturer may establish an informal dispute resolution program, and the settlement body may consider an award of attorney's fees to a successful consumer. *A state is also free to implement a lemon law requiring that all informal dispute settlement procedures comply with additional requirements imposed by state law (such as fee-shifting), but in many cases the state legislatures have not done so.*

In the case that follows—*Fedor v. Nissan of North America, Inc.*, 84 A.3d 601 (N.J. 2014)—the consumer was aware that unless otherwise agreed between the manufacturer and the consumer, the informal dispute resolution program would not address attorney's fees.

The award was rendered, addressing the consumer's grievance and requiring repurchase of the defective vehicle. Fedor accepted the award, knowing that it was final and that it did not provide for an award of attorney's fees.

The court rejected the consumer's suggestion that failure to award attorney's fees in every instance would encourage and increase litigation. The consumer's acceptance of the informal dispute settlement decision demonstrated their satisfaction with the forum, and the consumer did not reject the award of repurchase in favor of initiating legal action in the hope of also collecting attorney's fees.

On January 10, 2009, Gene Fedor purchased a new 2009 Nissan Quest minivan for the sum of $30,289.00.

The Nissan warranty that came with the vehicle required dissatisfied consumers to first file claims with BBB Auto Line, an informal automotive complaint resolution program independently operated by the Council of Better Business Bureaus, Inc.

BBB Auto Line attempted to assist the consumer in resolving vehicle problems. If mediation was unsuccessful, the consumer then had the opportunity to present the claims to an arbitrator. Neither the consumer nor the manufacturer was legally bound by the arbitrator's decision unless accepted by the consumer. The arbitrator could award all available state lemon law remedies "excluding attorney's fees, any penalties, or multiple damages."

As a result of recurring problems with the minivan—all of which remained unresolved despite numerous attempts to repair them—Fedor filed a lawsuit against Nissan on June 15, 2011, some two and a half years after he purchased the vehicle. Fedor alleged violations of the state lemon law and the federal Magnuson–Moss Act.

Following discovery, Nissan moved to dismiss the Magnuson–Moss Act cause of action due to Fedor's failure to utilize Nissan's informal dispute settlement procedure through BBB Auto Line, as required by the warranty.

Fedor objected, contending that the BBB Auto Line program mandated by Nissan's warranty did not comply with state and federal law because it failed to include an award of attorney's fees to a successful consumer.

Fedor's warranty claims were then submitted to BBB Auto Line, and an arbitration was conducted on December 21, 2011. The arbitrator concluded that Fedor was entitled to a repurchase of his vehicle by Nissan.

Fedor executed the Acceptance or Rejection of Decision form, accepting the arbitrator's decision by checking the provision of the agreement that stated: "I ACCEPT THE ARBITRATION DECISION. I understand this means I will be legally bound, which means I give up any right to sue the business in court on any claim that has been resolved at the arbitration hearing, unless otherwise provided by state or federal law."

Notwithstanding his acceptance of the arbitration decision, Fedor insisted that he was entitled to an award of attorney's fees. Fedor first requested a fee-shifting hearing through the BBB Auto Line program, but Nissan refused to participate. Fedor then sought judicial redress under his previously filed complaint. and the matter proceeded through nonbinding, court-ordered arbitration.

The arbitrator ruled in favor of Nissan, finding that attorneys' fees were neither authorized under the informal dispute resolution program nor mandated as a matter of law. Nissan then moved for summary judgment, which was granted by the court.

On appeal, Fedor argued that the court "undervalued strong policy interests served by fee-shifting at informal dispute settlement procedures" and that the court incorrectly allowed Nissan's warranty dispute settlement procedure to be exempt from the requirements of the lemon law.

Fedor also contended that the court erred in concluding there was no state cause of action allowing fee-shifting "for consumers who prevailed at an informal dispute settlement procedure under the Magnuson–Moss Act." As a result, Fedor sought an order reinstating his claims for attorney's fees and costs.

The Magnuson–Moss Act, the court explained, was enacted to assist motor vehicle owners complaining that manufacturers and dealers were not honoring their warranties, and the statute imposed federal minimum standards for product warranties. The act also required manufacturers to "fully and conspicuously disclose" the terms of coverage "in simple and readily understood language."

The Magnuson–Moss Act provided a cause of action for consumers harmed by a warrantor's failure to comply with its obligations whereby consumer disputes could be expeditiously settled through informal dispute settlement mechanisms at little or no cost to the consumer.

The act apparently was not very effective though, and many states enacted lemon laws to establish the rights and duties of manufacturers, dealers, and consumers regarding the repair and return of defective motor vehicles. Lemon laws were designed to aid consumers in their efforts to enforce automobile warranties.

The threefold purpose of the state lemon laws was to:

- Require the manufacturer of a new motor vehicle to correct defects originally covered under warranty which are identified and reported within a specified period,
- Provide procedures to expeditiously resolve disputes between a consumer and a manufacturer when defects in a new motor vehicle were not corrected within a reasonable time, and
- Award specific remedies where the uncorrected defect substantially impairs the use, value, or safety of the new motor vehicle.

To effectuate these objectives, the lemon laws imposed an affirmative obligation on the vehicle manufacturer to repair substantial defects within a reasonable time. If the manufacturer was unable to repair the vehicle within the statutory timeframe, the consumer was entitled to a full refund of the purchase price of the vehicle in addition to any other charges or fees associated with the ownership of the vehicle. The manufacturer could offer to replace the vehicle in lieu of a refund, but the consumer was free to reject such offer and demand a refund.

To assert a claim under the lemon law, a consumer had to report the claimed nonconformity to the manufacturer or its dealer within the earlier of the first 24,000 miles of operation or two years following the date of delivery of the vehicle. Following the report of a nonconformity to the manufacturer, the manufacturer had three attempts or a cumulative total of 30 calendar days, whichever occurred first, to repair the nonconforming vehicle.

If the manufacturer or its dealer was unable to repair or correct the nonconformity, the consumer was entitled to return the vehicle to the manufacturer and receive a full refund of the purchase price, along with any other charges or fees associated with the vehicle's ownership, less a reasonable allowance for vehicle use.

The state's lemon law identified three forums to resolve disputes between a consumer and a manufacturer, including a manufacturer's informal dispute resolution procedure, if one was established. The law specifically referenced the informal dispute settlement procedures offered by the manufacturers pursuant to the Magnuson–Moss Act.

The statute provided in pertinent part:

a. If a manufacturer has established an informal dispute settlement procedure pursuant to the Magnuson–Moss Act a consumer may submit a dispute regarding motor vehicle nonconformities to the dispute settlement body provided by that procedure, but a consumer *shall not be required to first participate in the informal dispute settlement procedure* before participating in the summary hearing procedure under this act.

b. If a consumer chooses to use a manufacturer's informal dispute settlement procedure, the findings of the dispute settlement body shall state in writing whether the consumer is entitled to a refund, and the findings shall be admissible in any legal action.

c. If the dispute settlement body determines that a consumer is entitled to relief under this act, the consumer shall be entitled to a refund as authorized by the state's lemon law.

d. In any informal dispute settlement procedure established pursuant to this section:

❖ ❖ ❖

(4) If the dispute settlement body rules in favor of the consumer, his costs and reasonable attorney's fees shall also be awarded. (Emphasis added)

Thus, under the lemon law statute, an aggrieved consumer was not required to participate in a manufacturer's informal dispute settlement procedure before filing suit, but a consumer was to be awarded reasonable attorney's fees if the consumer was successful in a lawsuit.

Fedor argued that the use of a manufacturer's informal dispute resolution mechanism could not prevent an award of attorney's fees, a remedy allowed under both the Magnuson–Moss Act and the lemon law. Fedor also contended that any informal dispute settlement procedure that alleged compliance with the Magnuson–Moss Act must include attorney's fee-shifting, and the consumers' rights should not be reduced because they accepted relief in arbitration.

The appellate court, first of all, rejected Fedor's assertion that a warrantor's informal dispute resolution mechanism adopted under the Magnuson–Moss Act, such as Auto Line, was required to include a fee-shifting component for successful consumers. The court concluded that the statute and its regulations provided otherwise.

Second, the court saw no justification for the assertion that attorney's fees could be recovered under the lemon law by a consumer who elected to accept relief awarded through a manufacturer's informal dispute resolution mechanism created under the Magnuson–Moss Act.

In fact, Nissan's warranty and its informal dispute resolution mechanism *excluded* attorney fee awards, a consequence clearly foreseen by the Magnuson–Moss Act. Attorneys' fees were only available to consumers who prevailed in an action before the court.

Fedor's policy argument—allowing informal dispute resolution mechanisms to deny attorney fee awards will encourage consumers to choose litigation—ignored the benefits provided by alternative dispute resolution forums, including:

- No filing fees or costs for the consumer,
- Proceedings tailored to *pro se* representation and no legal representation required,
- Inspection of the vehicle and all complaint records by an independent expert at no cost to the consumer,
- Swift decisions unburdened by the formality of court processes, and
- Nonbinding resolution, with ability to initiate full judicial review.

The terms of participation in the BBB Auto Line program were clearly expressed and emphasize the objective of facilitating communication between consumers and warrantors to assure compliance with warranty provisions. It was undisputed that this forum excluded other claims made by the consumer, including demands for attorney's fees.

In this light, the court concluded that Congress encouraged the creation of informal dispute resolution mechanisms by warrantors to give consumers quick, yet effective, relief, without requiring these mechanisms to mimic legal redress. The absence of an attorney fee award neither violated the statute and its regulations nor offended public policy. Use of informal dispute resolution mechanisms was a compromise between consumers and warrantors.

Utilization of Auto Line was required prior to filing suit under the Magnusson–Moss Act, but it was not a prerequisite to an action under the lemon law. Fedor chose to use the warranty-provided informal dispute resolution program conducted by Auto Line, knowing that it expressly stated that attorney's fees are not awarded. Fedor also accepted the Auto Line award granting repurchase of the defective vehicles, and he was aware that by doing so he agreed to forego the opportunity to file suit.

Fedor was free to reject the Auto Line award and proceed with a private right of action for breach of warranty in the hope of obtaining additional relief, including attorney's fees. However, by electing to accept the informal dispute settlement determination of repurchase, Fedor waived all further remedies under the Magnuson–Moss Act. Fedor also argued that the lemon law imposed a nonwaivable attorney's fee-shifting requirement on informal dispute settlement procedures.

Fedor reasoned that the lemon law incorporates the informal dispute settlement procedures of the Magnuson–Moss Act as minimum standards and therefore require attorney's fee-shifting. The court, however, rejected this line of argument, as it too ignored the plain language of the statute.

The court concluded that the specific use of two distinct provisions to discuss informal dispute resolution programs reflected the legislature's recognition of two separate informal dispute settlement forums: those established pursuant to the Magnuson–Moss Act and those designed to comply with the lemon law. The court's conclusion was further reinforced by the language of other sections of the statute.

If an informal dispute resolution program was established by a manufacturer under the lemon law, the settlement body had to consider an award of attorney's fees to a successful consumer. However, the lemon law did not impose a universal requirement for a fee award in any other informal dispute resolution programs, including those established under the Magnuson–Moss Act.

In this case, the BBB Auto Line was created under the Magnuson–Moss Act, not the state lemon law.

Fedor contended that if the lemon law provides for attorney's fees in some circumstances, such as administrative proceedings and informal dispute settlement procedures established under the lemon law, then attorney's fees must be available under all circumstances, including resolution by an informal dispute settlement mechanism established pursuant to the Magnuson–Moss Act. Fedor asserted that the manufacturer's informal dispute resolution mechanism "must still comply with and offer remedies afforded by the host state's lemon laws."

The court rejected this proposition, as Fedor did not offer any authority that the lemon law, as a matter of public policy, was intended to allow an award of attorney's fees to consumers utilizing a manufacturer's informal dispute settlement procedure, even one established pursuant to the Magnuson–Moss Act.

The court further noted that the state's lemon law did not impose upon all manufacturers who offered an informal dispute resolution mechanism a requirement to comply with the statute. While a state is free to implement a lemon law requiring all informal dispute settlement procedures, including those established pursuant to the Magnuson–Moss

Act, to comply with additional requirements imposed by state law (such as fee-shifting), the state legislature had not done so.

The court made a final observation. The Magnuson–Moss Act and the state lemon law were aimed at addressing the types of manufacturing defects experienced by consumers. The procedures were fully explained in the statutes and regulations. In this matter, further instructions governing the BBB Auto Line program were provided.

Fedor was aware that unless otherwise agreed between the manufacturer and the consumer, Auto Line would not address attorney's fees. The Auto Line award was rendered, addressing consumers' grievances and in both cases requiring repurchase of the defective vehicles. Fedor accepted the award, knowing that it was final and that it did not provide for an award of fees.

The court rejected Fedor's suggestion that failure to award fees in every instance would encourage and increase litigation. His acceptance of the informal dispute settlement decision demonstrated his satisfaction with the forum, and he did not reject the award of repurchase in favor of initiating legal action in the hope of also collecting attorney's fees.

Policy arguments advanced by consumers in favor of fee-shifting, the court stated, would be better directed to the legislature than the judiciary.

Appendix A

State Lemon Laws

The following is a list of statutory references to state lemon laws:

State	Statute
Alabama	Title 8, Chapter 20A: Secs. 8-20A-1 to 8-20A-6
Alaska	Title 45, Ch. 45: 45.45.300 to 45.45.360
Arizona	Title 44, Ch. 9, Art. 5; 44-1261–44-1267
Arkansas	Title 4, Subtitle 7, Ch. 90: Subchapter 4: 4-90-401 to 4-90-417
California	CA Civil Code Title 1.7 Ch. 1, Ch.1.5
Colorado	Title 42, Art. 10: Secs. 42-10-101 to 42-10-107
Connecticut	Title 42, Ch. 743b; 42-179 to 42-180
Delaware	Title 6, Subtitle II, Ch. 50: Sections 5001-5009
District of Columbia	DC Code § 50-502
Florida	Title XXXIX, Ch. 681: Sections 681.10 to 681.118
Georgia	10-1-780 to 10-1-792
Hawaii	Title 26, Chapter 481I: Sections 481I-1 to 481I-4
Idaho	Title 48, Ch. 9: Sections 48-901 to 48-913
Illinois	Volume 815, Code 380, Sections 1-8
Indiana	Title 24, Article 5, Chapter 13 and 13.5: Sections 244-5-13-1 to 24-5-13.5-14
Iowa	Chapter 322G: Sections 22G.1 to 322G.15
Kansas	Chapter 50, Article 6: Sec. 50-645
Kentucky	Chapter 367: Sections 367.840 to 367.846

State	Statute
Louisiana	Title 51: Sections 51:1941 to 51:1949
Maine	Title 10, Chapter 203-A: 1161 to 1169
Maryland	Commercial Law: 14-1501 to 14-1504
Massachusetts	Chapter 90, Section 7N to Section 7N1/2
Michigan	MCL 257.1401 to 257.1410
Minnesota	Chapter 325F: Section 665
Mississippi	Title 63, Chapter 17: Sections 63-17-151 to 63-17-165
Missouri	Title XXVI, Chapter 407: Sections 407.560 to 407.583
Montana	Title 61, Chapter 4, Part 5: 61-4-501 to 61-4-526
Nebraska	Chapter 60: Secs. 60-2701 to 60-2709
Nevada	N.R.S.587-600-597-680 – Lemon Law Nevada Revised Statutes–Actions by Victims of Fraud
New Hampshire	Title 31, Chapter 357-D: 357-D:1 to 357-D:12
New Jersey	Title 56, Chapter 12: 56:12-29 to 56:12-49
New Mexico	Chapter 57, Article 16A; 57-16A-1 to 57-16A-9
New York	General Business, Article 11-A, Sections 198-a and 198-b
North Carolina	Chapter 20, Article 15A, Sections 20-351 to 20-351.10
North Dakota	Sections 51-07-16–51-07-22
Ohio	Title 13, Section 1345, part 1345.71 to 1345.77
Oklahoma	Title 15, Chapter 22: Section 15-901
Oregon	ORS 646A.400-646A.418
Pennsylvania	Title 73, Chapter 28: Sec. 1951–1963
Rhode Island	Title 31, Chapter 31-5.2: Sections 31-5.2-1 to 31-5.2-13
South Carolina	Title 56, Chapter 28, Sections 10-110; 56-28-10 to 56-28-110
South Dakota	Title 32, Chapter 6D, Sections 1 thru 11: 32-6D-1 to 32-6D-11
Tennessee	Title 55 Chapter 24 Section 101-112
Texas	Title 43 Part 10 Chapter 215 subsection G
Utah	Title 13, Chapter 20, Sections 1-7; 13-20-1 to 13-20-7

State	Statute
Vermont	Title 9, Part 4, Chapter 115, Sections 4170-4181
Virginia	Title 59.1, Chapter 17.3: Sections 207.9-207.16:1;59.1-207.9 to 59.1-207.16:1
Washington	Title 19, Chapter 118: Sections 19.118.005 to 19.118.170
West Virginia	Chapter 46A, Article 6A: 46A-6A-1 to 46A-6A-9
Wisconsin	Chapter 218: Sec. 218.0171
Wyoming	Title 40, Chapter 17, Sec. 101

The Center for Auto Safety also has a helpful website on lemon laws: https://www.autosafety.org/state-lemon-law-criteria/

As does the Tesla corporation: https://www.tesla.com/sites/default/files/blog_attachments/ownersrightsnotification.pdf

Appendix B

Model Petition

The following is an example of a lemon law complaint:

JOHN DOE,	§	IN THE DISTRICT COURT OF
	§	
Plaintiff,	§	
v.	§	TRAVIS COUNTY, TEXAS
TESLA, INC. d/b/a	§	55TH JUDICIAL DISTRICT
TESLA MOTORS, INC.	§	
	§	
Defendant.	§	
	§	
	§	
	§	
	§	

PLAINTIFF'S ORIGINAL PETITION

TO THE HONORABLE JUDGE OF SAID COURT:

NOW COMES JOHN DOE, hereinafter referred to as Plaintiff, complaining of and about TESLA, INC. d/b/a TESLA MOTORS, INC. ("Defendant Tesla"), hereinafter referred to as Defendant, and for cause of action show the Court the following:

DISCOVERY CONTROL PLAN LEVEL

1. Plaintiff seeks monetary relief of $100,000.00 or less, exclusive of costs, interest, and attorney fees, and intends that discovery be conducted under Discovery Level 3.

PARTIES AND SERVICE

2. Plaintiff JOHN DOE is an individual residing in Travis County, Texas.
3. Defendant, TESLA, INC. d/b/a TESLA MOTORS, INC., is a foreign profit corporation with a principal place of business located at 3500 Deer Creek Road, Palo Alto, California 94304. Upon information and belief, TESLA, INC. d/b/a TESLA MOTORS, INC. is authorized to do business in Texas. This Defendant may be served with process by serving its registered agent, CT Corporation System, 701 Brazos St # 720, Austin, TX 78701.

JURISDICTION AND VENUE

4. The subject matter in controversy is within the jurisdictional limits of this court.
5. This court has jurisdiction over the parties because Defendant Tesla does business in Texas.
6. Venue in Travis County is proper in this cause under Section 15.002(a)(4) of the Texas Civil Practice and Remedies Code because the Defendant is a non-resident of the state of Texas.

FACTS

7. On or about January 10, 2021, Plaintiff purchased a new 2021 Tesla Model S, VIN 5YJSA1E22GF176266 (the "Subject Vehicle") from an Authorized Dealership. Please see Exhibit A: Purchase Agreement.
8. The Subject Vehicle is registered in the State of Texas and was purchased primarily for personal, family, and/or household purposes.
9. At the time of purchase, the Subject Vehicle was accompanied by a factory warranty which, in relevant part, provided for a four (4) year/50,000 mile New Vehicle Limited Warranty and eight (8) year Battery and Drive Unit Warranty (the "Warranty"). Please see Exhibit B: Pertinent Portion of Warranty. Warranty in its entirety is in Defendant's possession.
10. Defendant Tesla's warranties covered any repairs or replacements needed during the warranty period and/or due to defects in factory materials or workmanship.

11. In fact, when delivered, the Subject Vehicle was defective in materials and workmanship, such defects being discovered within the warranty periods and repairs were attempted. Shortly after purchase, Plaintiff noticed numerous defects in the Subject Vehicle, including, but not limited to: (1) The Subject Vehicle repeatedly pulls to the right despite numerous repair attempts, (2) The steering column of Subject Vehicle pulls to the left despite numerous repair attempts, (3) The Subject Vehicle contains numerous battery defects, (4) The air conditioning of Subject Vehicle malfunctions, despite numerous repair attempts, (5) The chiller expansion valve of Subject Vehicle is faulty, (6) The cabin of the Subject Vehicle is subject to wind sound at highway speeds, (7) The touchscreen of the Subject Vehicle goes blank during operation, (8) A noticeable gap appears on the driver side A-pillar seal at the door frame of the Subject Vehicle, (9) The TPMS (Tire Pressure Monitoring System) of the Subject Vehicle is faulty, and (10) the driver and passenger side lower interior B-pillar trim of the Subject Vehicle is loose. Plaintiff returned the vehicle to an Authorized Dealership for repair on at least eight (8) occasions. Please see Exhibit C: Repair Orders.
12. Authorized Dealership has test driven the vehicle and made repairs to the vehicle, however, the defects continue to exist. During said repairs the Subject Vehicle was out of service for at least twenty-eight (28) days.
13. Despite the prolonged time during which Defendant was given the opportunity to repair Plaintiff's Vehicle, Defendant failed to repair the Subject Vehicle so as to bring it into conformity with the warranties set forth herein.
14. The defects experienced by the Plaintiff with the Subject Vehicle substantially impaired its use, value and safety to the Plaintiff, and has shaken the Plaintiff's faith in the vehicle to operate as dependable transportation.
15. Despite Plaintiff's repeated efforts to allow Defendant the opportunity to repair the Subject Vehicle, many nonconforming and defective conditions were not repaired and still exist.
16. Plaintiff directly notified Defendant of the defective conditions concerning the Subject Vehicle and that Plaintiff desired a buy-back of the Subject Vehicle. Please see Exhibit D: Written Notification.

17. This cause of action arises out of the Defendant's breaches of warranty and contract and violations of the enclosed statutes, as set forth in this Complaint.
18. As a result, Plaintiff seeks to revoke his acceptance of the Subject Vehicle and be refunded the purchase price, along with all expenses Plaintiff has incurred as a result of the Subject Vehicle's nonconformities, including loss of use of the Subject Vehicle, and reimbursement for expenses related to aftermarket items installed on the Subject Vehicle.
19. In the alternative, Plaintiff seeks damages in the form of all expenses Plaintiff has incurred as a result of the Subject Vehicle's nonconformities, including loss of use of the Subject Vehicle, diminution of value of the Subject Vehicle, and costs of repair to return the vehicle to its warranted state, as well as reimbursement for expenses related to aftermarket items installed on the Subject Vehicle.

PLAINTIFF'S CLAIM OF BREACH OF WARRANTY

20. Plaintiff incorporates by reference all of the allegations set forth above.
21. Defendant Tesla extended to Plaintiff a four (4) year/50,000 mile New Vehicle Limited Warranty and eight (8) year Battery and Drive Unit Warranty ("Warranty").
22. Plaintiff, seeking to repair the Subject Vehicle, attempted to exercise his rights under the Warranty.
23. Defendant Tesla has failed to honor the terms of the Warranty.
24. As a result of the actions set forth above, Defendant Tesla has breached the Warranty.
25. As a result of Defendant Tesla's breach of Warranty, Plaintiff has and will continue to suffer significant monetary and consequential damages.

WHEREFORE, Plaintiff respectfully requests that this Honorable Court enter Judgment in favor of Plaintiff and against Defendant in an amount to be determined at the Trial of the matter, but believed to be monetary relief of $100,000.00 or less, exclusive of costs, interest and attorney fees.

PLAINTIFF'S CLAIM OF BREACH OF IMPLIED WARRANTY: TEXAS BUSINESS AND COMMERCE CODE SEC. 2.314

26. Plaintiff incorporates by reference all of the allegations set forth above.
27. The aforementioned Subject Vehicle purchased by Plaintiff was subject to implied warranties of merchantability under the Texas Business and Commerce Code – Section 2.314.
28. A warranty that goods shall be merchantable is implied in a contract for their sale if the seller is a merchant with respect to goods of that kind as stated in Texas Business and Commerce Code Section 2.314(1). Said implied warranties included, but are not limited to, the following:
    - **a.** Said Vehicle must pass without objection in the trade under the contract description; and
    - **b.** Said Vehicle must be of fair average quality; and
    - **c.** Said Vehicle must be fit for the ordinary purposes for which it is used.
29. Said Vehicle was not warranted and represented in that Defendant Tesla has failed and refused to repair any defects and nonconformities.
30. Plaintiff has given Defendant Tesla a reasonable opportunity to reinstate any and all warranties so as to cure any defects and nonconformities with the Subject Vehicle but Defendant Tesla has failed to do so within a reasonable time and without costs to Plaintiff.
31. As a result of Defendant Tesla's breach of implied warranties, Plaintiff has and will continue to suffer significant monetary damages.

WHEREFORE, Plaintiff respectfully requests that this Honorable Court enter Judgment in favor of Plaintiff and against Defendant Tesla in an amount to be determined at the Trial of the matter, but believed to be monetary relief of $100,000.00 or less, exclusive of costs, interest and attorney fees.

PLAINTIFF'S CLAIM OF BREACH OF THE MAGNUSON-MOSS WARRANTY ACT

32. Plaintiff incorporates by reference all of the allegations set forth above.
33. This Court has jurisdiction to decide claims brought under 15 USC § 2301 et seq., by virtue of 15 USC § 2310(d)(1)(A).
34. Plaintiff is a consumer as defined by 15 USC § 2301(3).
35. Defendant Tesla is supplier and warrantor as defined by 15 USC § 2301(4),(5).
36. The Subject Vehicle is a consumer product as defined by 15 USC § 2301(1).
37. 15 USC § 2301(6), requires Defendant Tesla, as a warrantor, to remedy any defects, malfunction or nonconformance of the Subject Vehicle within a reasonable time and without charge to Plaintiff, as defined in 15 USC § 2304(d).
38. The actions of Defendant Tesla as herein above described and in failing to tender the Subject Vehicle to Plaintiff free of defects and refusing to repair or replace the defective vehicle tendered to Plaintiff, constitute a breach of the written and implied warranties covering the Subject Vehicle and are a violation of the Magnuson-Moss Warranty Act.
39. Despite repeated demands and despite the fact that the Plaintiff has complied with all reasonable terms and conditions imposed upon her by Defendant Tesla, Defendant Tesla has failed and/or refused to cure any defects and nonconformity with the Subject Vehicle.
40. As a result of Defendant Tesla's breach of express and implied warranties as set forth above, and Defendant Tesla's failure to honor its obligations under its warranties, Plaintiff has and will continue to suffer damages as enumerated above.
41. Defendant Tesla has had a reasonable opportunity to remedy the defects in the vehicle but have failed to do so, thereby entitling Plaintiff to a refund of the purchase price pursuant to the Magnuson-Moss Warranty Act.
42. Pursuant to the Magnuson-Moss Warranty Act, 15 U.S.C. § 2310(d)(2), Plaintiff is entitled to recover as part of the judgment, costs and expenses of the suit including attorney's fees based on actual time expended.

WHEREFORE, Plaintiff prays that this Honorable Court enter an order requiring Defendant to accept return of the Subject Vehicle and refund Plaintiff the purchase price, together with any and all incidental and consequential damages, including attorney fees as provided by 15 USC § 2310(d)(2) and such other and further equitable relief to which Plaintiff is entitled. In the alternative, Plaintiff seeks damages in the form of all expenses Plaintiff has incurred as a result of the Subject Vehicle's nonconformities, including loss of use of the Subject Vehicle, diminution of value of the Subject Vehicle, and costs of repair to return the vehicle back to its warranted state.

PRAYER

WHEREFORE, PREMISES CONSIDERED, Plaintiff John Doe respectfully prays that the Defendant be cited to appear and answer herein, and that upon a final hearing of the cause, judgment be entered for the Plaintiff against Defendant for damages in an amount within the jurisdictional limits of the Court; at the maximum rate allowed by law; post-judgment interest at the legal rate; costs of court; attorney fees and costs; and such other and further relief to which the Plaintiff may be entitled at law or in equity.

Respectfully submitted,

LAW OFFICES OF LEMONT SMITH, PLLC

By: /s/ Lemont Smith
Lemont Smith
Texas State Bar No.: 2211760033
2500 Main Street Blvd., Suite 2100
Austin, Texas 77019
(222) 799-6822
lsmith@lslaw.com

PLAINTIFF HEREBY DEMANDS TRIAL BY JURY

About the Author

Cecil C. Kuhne III is a litigator in the Dallas office of Norton Rose Fulbright. After driving a series of lemons for years, he now finds that he actually prefers them.

Index